HEXAPOD STORIES

Books by
Edith M. Patch

NATURE STUDY

Dame Bug and Her Babies

Hexapod Stories

Bird Stories

First Lessons in Nature Study

Holiday Pond

Holiday Meadow

Holiday Hill

Holiday Shore

Mountain Neighbors

Desert Neighbors

Forest Neighbors

Prairie Neighbors

NATURE AND SCIENCE READERS

Hunting

Outdoor Visits

Surprises

Through Four Seasons

Science at Home

The Work of Scientists

HEXAPOD STORIES

by

Edith M. Patch

illustrated by

Robert J. Sim

YESTERDAY'S CLASSICS

ITHACA, NEW YORK

This edition, first published in 2018 by Yesterday's Classics, an imprint of Yesterday's Classics, LLC, is an unabridged republication of the text originally published by The Atlantic Monthly Press in 1920. For the complete listing of the books that are published by Yesterday's Classics, please visit www.yesterdaysclassics. com. Yesterday's Classics is the publishing arm of the Baldwin Online Children's Literature Project which presents the complete text of hundreds of classic books for children at www.mainlesson.com.

ISBN: 978-1-63334-100-5

Yesterday's Classics, LLC
PO Box 339
Ithaca, NY 14851

CONTENTS

TO
ALICE PATCH

TO INTRODUCE TWELVE LITTLE HEXAPODS

THE Hexapods are funny folk who have six feet. That is they have six when they are grown up, though some of the children have none at all, and some have as many as twenty-two. You can tell from this that they are strange people, and you may call them fairies if you like!

They have wings,—the grown-up ones do,—wonderful wings of many shapes and colors. Luna's wings are green,—pale, pale green,—and very lovely, with a purple border on them. Perhaps there is nothing more beautiful in the world than Luna's wings. When Van flies, you can see the yellow edge of her brown wings; and when she alights—hesto! presto! you can see nothing at all; for she disappears from sight even though she is near enough to touch. Carol wears her wings neatly folded like a fan, except when she is using them. And Gryl, the little black minstrel—oh, Gryl fiddles with his wings.

They do queer things that we could not do if we tried. Old Bumble sleeps for more than half a year, and then wakes, thinking nothing of it at all, as if that were the most natural way to take a nap. Keti starts to build

1

himself a log cabin before he is a day old; and finishes it, too, in time, with no one to show him how. And Cecid bewitches the willow with a magic no one else can learn.

Yes, you may call the Hexapods fairies, if you like; but you must never, never forget that they are every bit as real and true as you are, even if they are so very different.

They are not far away, not farther than the flowers or the trees or the nearest brook. And there are so many millions of them that every child in the world might have some for pets and they would never be missed.

And let me tell you this, for this is very important: although Hexapods are common and easy to find, there is not one among them all that does not have a story about his life so strange and interesting that he is worth watching just to find out what his story is.

Are you pleased to know that, whether you are in the country or in the city, and whether it is summer or winter, you are living right in the midst of Hexapod Land, where you have these most wonderful fairies for next-door neighbors?

EDITH M. PATCH.

Van was ready to enjoy a New Year's Dinner.

CHAPTER I

VAN, THE SLEEPY BUTTERFLY

Who Was Wakened by a January Thaw

VAN was having a happy time making her New Year's calls.

She had crept out of bed about noon, for there was no cold wind blowing, and the sun had thrown its warm rays against the loose piece of bark under which she was sleeping. These warm rays had wakened her. That was a pleasant way of starting January, to have the sun knock at her door with its own sort of "Happy New Year!"

Other pleasant things happened, too. To begin with, Van was thirsty; and there is much to enjoy in being hungry and thirsty if there is food and drink near by. She had had nothing to eat during November or December, as it had been too cold for two months to do anything but sleep; and she was ready now to enjoy a New Year's dinner.

So she must have been glad when she had some invitations to "come and have a feast." Of course these were not written in notes, and put into envelopes, and stamped, and brought her by Uncle Sam's post-man. Nor were they brought her by messenger boys who said in words, "You are invited to dine at Mrs. Appleby's." Those would have been silly ways, for Van was a butterfly, and what did she know about written or spoken invitations or dinner-bells?

But there was a way for all that to let her know the table was spread for her. And after all, what better way, when folk (either boys or butterflies) have been without food until they are hungry, than to be tempted by good smells?

The first invitation that the air brought Van was from an old apple tree that lived near the edge of the woods. My, my! what a good-smelling one it was! The apples had frozen on the ground, and now they had thawed and were soft, and the juice was like cider. Oh, oh! what a feast for a thirsty butterfly!

Other guests had been before her. Brother Rabbit had eaten there more than once. Mr. Fieldmouse had nibbled up half an apple and left a pile of crumbs in its place. And the birds? There was one that very minute pecking with its thick short bill at an apple that had caught in the branches. So bird and beast and butterfly were all made happy by the New Year's gift of the old apple tree.

The second invitation the air brought Van was from a maple tree that lived down the same lane not far away. This was such a good one that Van could hardly get there fast enough. She fluttered her wings in a hurry to get a quick start, and then sailed for a little way. Then she fluttered her wings again as if she wanted to get there before it was too late. And no wonder! For there was a broken branch on the maple and a little icicle where some sap had dripped out and had frozen, and now the icicle was melting. Maple syrup! Oh! oh! oh!

The third invitation that the air brought to Van was—But we shall never know because, just as she was starting to her third feast, a boy and a girl came racing down the lane.

"Oh, see!" they called; "a butterfly! A big beauty! Just think! A butterfly on New Year's Day! Let's take it home to show!" So they ran after Van, who was spreading her brown wings with yellow borders for a slow sail.

Oho! catch Van? Why they couldn't even see her! What had been a large butterfly, with wide showy wings, a minute before, now looked like a ragged bit of bark on a tree near by. Van had hidden. And she was almost near enough to touch, though perhaps a little too high. She had hidden right in plain sight. And all

Van now looked like a ragged bit of bark.

7

she had done was sit on the bark of the tree and fold her wings above her back and keep still. Catch Van? Why Van could fool a bird in a game of hide-and-seek!

By the time the children gave up the hunt, the sun was under a cloud and the wind felt chilly. So Van did not have any more feasting that day, or make any more New Year's calls. She was near her shelter of loose bark and crept up under cover out of the wind. She had had a good time. She had had cider and maple-sap enough to last her until the next thaw spell—be it one week or two, or one month, or two, or even three. Time was all alike to her when the weather was cold—short or long, it was the same! She just slept! You may ask the wisest man you know why it did Van no harm when the weather was cold as zero. If he is very wise, indeed, he will tell you, "I do not know why."

But our not knowing why made no difference to Van. She did live through the cold winter in the north, with no shelter but a loose bit of bark, just as her grandmother had lived one winter in a hollow tree, and her great-great-grandmother had lived under the roof of an old empty shed.

As spring came on, Van had invitations from the pussy willow, where she met some pretty flies with stripes on their bodies. She called, too, on the trailing arbutus, where she met Old Bumble more than once; for they both drank from those sweet pink cups and carried pollen from flower to flower.

Some time in May Van found that she could not spend all her time in calling on flowers, however much she liked their nectar, and however much they needed to have their pollen carried for them. So she hunted for a willow tree, and made a little ring around one of its twigs. This ring was set with fifty jewels, the very best she had to offer to the world. Of course, these jewels were her eggs.

In about two weeks they began to hatch, and Sister Essa was the very first of them all to bite around the edge of her egg-shell, until the top lifted like a little lid and out she came, looking much too long to be curled up in the shell she crept out of.

Essa did not go away from her brother and sister caterpillars. When they were all hatched, they crept off together and lay in a row side by side, with their heads at the edge of the leaf. There they had their breakfast, which it took them several days to eat.

And what do you suppose it was? No, their mother did not bring them cider from old soft apples, or syrup from broken maple twigs, or nectar from flowers. She was not like Old Bumble, who fed her babies every day. Van did not bring her fifty children one single thing to eat. Sister Essa was hungry, too; and so were the rest of the family. And here they were left on a willow branch, where there was nothing at all but leaves—food their mother never could have eaten with her long tongue, if she had uncoiled it and tried.

But we needn't worry about those babies. In less than the flick of a minute Sister Essa had nibbled a tiny green bite out of the top of the willow leaf, nodding her little head over it as her jaws opened and shut as if there

9

were nothing better to be had for a breakfast. All her brothers and sisters were nodding their heads just the same way, and while they were about it, they nibbled off the whole top of the leaf just as if it were a green layer cake and they wanted only the shiny frosting. Before breakfast was over, Sister Essa led them to another leaf, where they lay side by side in a row as before, and ate until their skins were too tight to hold another bit of shiny green frosting.

That was a sign that their breakfast was over; so they spun a thin mat with silk which they spilled out of a little tube near their lower lips, and took a nap on the mat.

The first day they rested quietly, but the second day they acted as if they were having bad dreams and tossed their heads a great deal. In fact Sister Essa jerked so hard at last that her little skull came off like an empty shell. By that time she was wide-awake, and crept out of her tight skin through the collar-hole the skull left when it tumbled off. Before she had time to turn around, all her brothers and sisters were jerking their skulls off, too, and creeping out of their skins through the collar-hole.

Something funny had happened to them and they never looked the same again. They now had new heads, with bigger jaws and fine new stretchy skins.

After that nap that had had such a queer end, they were hungry; so they went off to some new leaves (this time one was not big enough to hold them all) and lay in rows and ate their luncheon. It was so good they did not stop for nearly a week. When their luncheon was over at last, they spun another thin silk mat and had another nap. They woke in about two days, jerking their skulls off again, and crept through the collar-hole in their skins just as they had before. They now had still bigger heads, and skins that were stretchier than ever.

Well, that was the way Sister Essa went on doing, until she had had her dinner and another luncheon and her supper. Each meal lasted several days, with a day or two for a nap in between. Every time she wakened, she pushed and jerked inside her old skin, until her skull fell off like an empty nut-shell; and when she crept out of the collar-hole she looked different from the way she looked when she went to sleep.

By the time she was eating her supper, her skin was a soft black color, with little white specks like a "pepper-and-salt" suit. Down the middle of her back was a row of pretty red spots, and growing all over her sides were black spines with pointed branches. She was now two inches long and a fine-looking caterpillar—after one got used to seeing her.

As her brothers and sisters had all had the same sort of time growing that she had had, they were fine-looking, too, and so big that the fifty of them together made the tip of the willow branch hang down. They ate more for this meal than for any other, and they did not nibble just the shiny frosting as they did at breakfast when they were tiny—they gobbled up all the flat green cakes on the branch. This would have been a bad thing for a little tree which needed all its leaves to grow with.

11

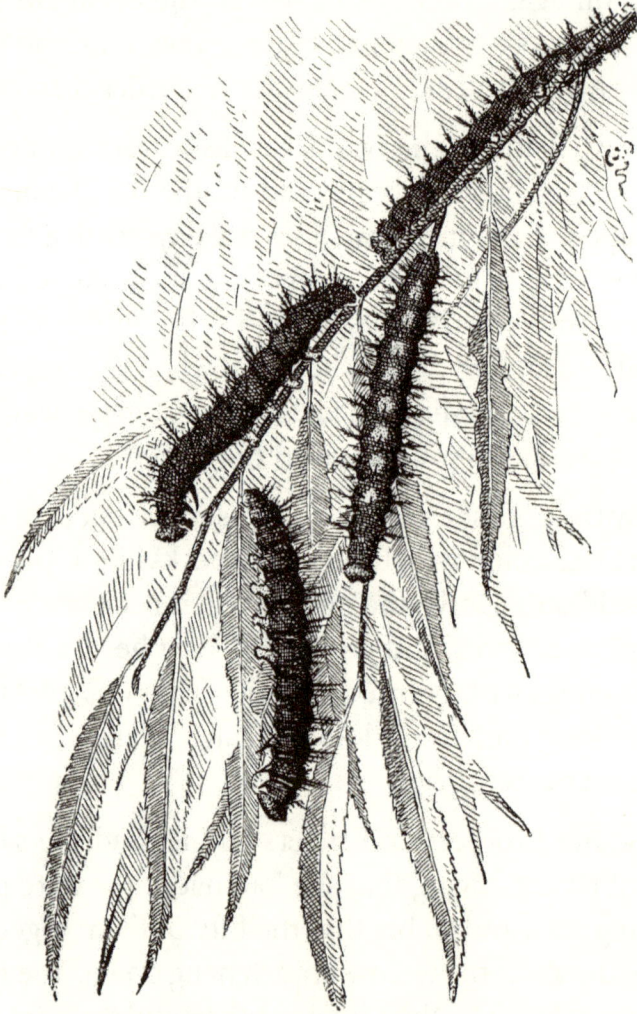

Each meal lasted several days.

Of course, if they had been on a small tree, it would have been better to take them off. But this was a big, big one, forty years old, and it was growing wild near a brook, with no gardener to trim off some of its branches; and what leaves Essa and the others ate could be spared as well as not. Of course, their supper must be a hearty one, for it had to last them until they were butterflies, like Van, with a long tongue to uncoil when calling on the flowers to sip nectar and to carry pollen.

You never would think, to look at Essa, that she would ever fly; for there she sat clinging to the branch with ten of her feet and drawing the edge of the leaf down to her mouth with her other six feet, and she didn't have a sign of wings anywhere on her back.

Ah, but Essa could do several things you would never think she could! She had never done them before—why should she now? You might not think she could creep head first down the trunk of the tree, and take a walk, as fast as she could hurry, along the ground, until she came to an old fence; and climb the fence, and spin a silk peg on the lower edge of a board, and fasten her hind-legs to the silk peg, and let go with all her other legs, and hang there head-down until her skull split and her skin ripped down the back seam!

You wouldn't know how Essa could do that, would you? And if you ask the wisest man you see *how* a caterpillar can do wonderful things like that just once in her life, without learning or without any one to show her about making a silk peg, maybe he will tell you he doesn't know, either.

But our not knowing how she can do it made no difference to Essa. That is just what she did when she had finished her supper; and while she was about it, she changed into a chrysalis, which looked no more like a butterfly than it did like a caterpillar.

There they hung on their silk pegs.

Well, there they hung, Essa and her forty-nine funny brother and sister chrysalids, for about ten days; and none of them knew anything about Lampy's fireworks on the Fourth o' July. Soon after that Essa broke her chrysalis case, and tumbled out head first. She didn't tumble far, for her feet caught hold of the empty case, and she hung there with her soft little wings down, until they grew big and stopped throbbing. She clung with four feet; but you must not think she had no more feet than a cat or a dog, for her first pair were folded against her breast and covered up by her pretty brown fur.

Some people said Essa's wings were purple, and some said they were brown. I don't know what you would think about their color. But all agreed that the border was pale yellow, and that next the yellow on the upper side was a dark band with lovely pale blue spots on it. And everybody who saw her said that she was a very beautiful butterfly when she spread her wings open, and that, when she folded them shut above her back, she looked like a piece of bark.

Essa flew about and made calls on the flowers, for there was flower nectar instead of frozen apple-cider in July. After a time she made a ring about the twig of a tree all set with her egg-jewels. I have forgotten whether she chose a willow or an elm; but it made no difference which, for her daughter Opie, when she hatched, could eat either one. If it had been an oak, Opie would have starved to death; but of course Essa would not have left her eggs on an oak or a pine tree.

Well, Opie and her brother and sister caterpillars ate and napped and grew, and changed into chrysalids and then into butterflies, just as their mother and their uncles and aunts had done.

But by this time it was the fall of the year, and Opie found her life much more like her grandmother's than it was like her mother's; for Essa had been a summer butterfly and Opie, like Van, was a winter one. So she flew about and called on the fall flowers, and when the days grew cold, she found a shelter as her grandmother Van had done, and went to sleep, clinging with four feet to the roof of her winter bedroom and folding the other two close to her breast.

There she rested all the winter long, except when the days were warm enough to thaw her out. For be it one month or three or even four, time was all alike to her when the weather was cold—short or long, it was all the same. Opie just slept!

15

CHAPTER II

OLD BUMBLE

CANDLEMAS DAY was bright and fair.

Perhaps the ground-hog came out of his hole and was scared by his shadow and went back to bed again. I do not know.

But I know Old Bumble didn't come out of her hole that day. Her legs were all cramped up with the cold, and even her pretty black and yellow fur couldn't keep her warm.

You see, she had chosen to make her winter bedroom in a little cave on the north side of a dry bank, and the sunshine did not touch it. This did very well last August when she went to bed. If she had been in a sunny place then, it might have been too hot for her. It didn't take much to disturb her when she first went to sleep. If anything had got into her bedroom then and touched her, she would have shaken herself and gone away and found or made a new place. In August she was what is called "a very light sleeper," and couldn't bear to be touched.

In winter she was different. If the ground-hog

had pawed her cave open and rolled her out of bed on Candlemas Day, she would not have known anything about it!

He didn't, so there she slept, though she had been napping for six months already and would very likely keep at it for two or three more. Isn't that pretty lazy for a bee?

Old Bumble's long nap.

She had not done one bit of work before she went to bed, either—that is, nothing except to straighten out her bedroom a little; and as that was hardly more than a hole in the ground, the process did not take her long. She had not even hunted for her own dinner, which was to last her all winter. She helped herself to some fresh honey that her older sisters had put into a honey-mug, and drank enough to fill her honey-sack, and then went off and crept into bed. Pretty lazy for a bee, wasn't she?

She not only slept through Candlemas Day, but St. Valentine's Day came, with its pretty shower of

17

cards and letters, and she didn't wake up then. George Washington's birthday found her sleeping still; and she didn't even dream while people were putting green ribbons in their buttonholes on St. Patrick's Day.

It was not, I think, until April that she first roused herself and poked her sleepy head out of doors. Perhaps she was a little April Fool, for there was not much that she could do so early in the spring.

Maybe, though, she could find something to drink, to make her feel better after her nap of many months. Yes, the cool wind brought her a sweet smell from the trailing arbutus, the loveliest blossom that grows in the spring. For Old Bumble lived in a land where people had not yet robbed the woods of this dear flower, which used to be very common in the days of your grandfathers, and is getting to be so rare that, unless you and the rest of us are careful, there will not be any left at all for your grandchildren to see.

Well, Old Bumble found a few of the very earliest pink sprays in the sunny places, and she sang a happy humming song as she sipped at the tiny sweet cups.

She did not stay up very long that day, for the sun soon went under a cloud and she felt like going to bed again. Then for a week or so it rained, so she took a nap until the weather was fine. After that, she got up and sipped from the different spring flowers as they blossomed, but still slept through the colder days.

Did anyone ever tell you that a bee is a busy little thing?

Well, you see how Old Bumble spent the greater part of the year just dozing the time away. But wait and see what she did the rest of her days!

As soon as the weather was warm enough she started out on a hunting trip. She buzzed slowly along near the ground, but this time it wasn't flowers she was after. She was house-hunting. Just bedrooms no longer suited her. She was done with sleeping day after day. What she wanted now was a nursery. She must find a place where she could bring up a family of children.

So here and there, and there and here, she flew, singing her slow hunting song as she went. Now and then she stopped and peeped into a hole, to see if she liked it; and if it was not good enough for her home, she came out and hunted still farther.

At last she found a place that would do nicely for her nursery. It was a home a field-mouse had lived in once upon a time, and a field-mouse has very good taste about underground houses. Any way, Old Bumble liked the same kind.

Of course it needed tidying up a bit after being empty so long. So she went right to house-cleaning as if she knew all about it. She had never done such a thing in her life before, but she was not so stupid that she had to be shown how to do everything. She had a way of getting things right the first time she tried. She had saved her strength for many months, and now she was going to use it.

Her nursery must be just exactly right! For one thing, it should be dry; and this empty mouse-hole had grown damp. So she worked about in the part she was going to use, and dried it out with the warmth of her body. She found the softest bits the mother mouse had left there, and shook them up with her jaws and piled them in a heap. Right in the very middle of this she hollowed out a little room, which covered her up, top and all, except a hole at one side which she kept for a doorway into her snug little nursery.

How Bumble's nest looked inside.

Then off she flew to the flowers for yellow pollen, which she gathered and packed into her pollen baskets on her hind legs. She brought back her load and put a lump of this yellow stuff, made moist and sweet with honey, right on the floor of her nursery. Next she brushed some wax off her body and made a little nest of it big enough for a few eggs.

Before night came on, she brushed off some more wax, and this she made into a honey-mug just inside her doorway, and into this she put what honey she had had time to gather.

But she must not fly too late, for her eggs must not get cold. If they did, it would take them longer to hatch, and she needed her daughters to help her as soon as could be. She sat on the little wax nest to keep it warm, and left it only long enough to fill her honey-mug, so that she could eat from it in the night or on stormy days. For, though she could sleep all winter without eating, she needed food now to give her strength.

In a few days her eggs hatched, and then she was busy as a mother robin feeding her young. They were white little babies without hair or legs, and you never could guess to look at one that it would some day be a black-and-yellow furry bee. You could not take a peep at them, though, as you can at little birds, because their nest had a tight wax cover, and the nest was in the nursery, and the nursery was in a hole, and the hole was in the ground.

Now, how could Old Bumble feed her little ones if she kept them shut up tight in bag of wax? Well, for part of their food they ate up the pollen paste she kept bringing and sticking close against their nest.

But that wasn't all they had to eat. Their mother mixed some pollen with honey until it was thin, and then bit a hole in the top of the nest and dropped it from her mouth. Every time she did this, she mended with wax the hole she made, for her babies had to be kept shut up tight.

You can see that, with getting pollen and nectar

from the flowers, and making pollen-paste and honey for the children, and brushing wax from her body to use in keeping the nest and honey-mug mended, and storing honey in the honey-mug for nights and stormy days, the mother bee was not so lazy as she seemed at first. We might call her a very busy Old Bumble, indeed. A happy one, too, humming her cheerful song as she flew about on her out-door errands.

Old Bumble and a son and daughter bee.

In eleven or twelve days the little ones stopped eating and each one spun a thin cocoon about herself, for she must still be covered up. This would seem to give their mother a chance to rest. But no! It only meant new duties. She must clean away the wax and pollen from the cocoons, and make new wax nests and lay more eggs. Besides, she must keep the cocoons warm. So she spread her furry body out as big as she could make it stretch, like a mother biddy covering her little ones under her feathers.

After about two weeks, or maybe it was not quite so long, the young bees began to bite holes in the caps of their cocoons, which might make you think of chickens pipping their shells. They had had enough of being shut up. They were now coming out into the world. This time Old Bumble did not try to wax them in. She helped them out. She might well be glad to see her daughters, even though they were queer and feeble little things. Their fur was as wet as a chicken's down when it first comes out of the shell. Their legs were so weak they could hardly toddle over to the honey-mug for their breakfast. After they had eaten, they crept back and cuddled down under their mother, until their fur was dry and fluffy and they felt strong.

Only a few days more, and Old Bumble's daughters were ready to help her. Good, faithful, cheery Old Bumble—her pretty wings had grown tattered and torn with her flying for food. Her fur coat, that was so fresh and fine, was now looking ragged. But the little daughters that snuggled up close to her soon began to do her flying, and she could stay at home and keep house and rest her tired wings.

What was this stir and bustle about the nursery? Why, Hum and Buzz were ready to start out on their first journey. And little Flyaway was going, too. They looked much as their mother did when she left her bedroom, only much, much smaller. As their sisters were not quite ready yet to fly, they stayed at home and helped Hum and Buzz and Flyaway, when they came back, to feed the baby sisters that hatched from the eggs Old Bumble laid while they were spinning their cocoons.

23

*Hum and Buzz were ready to start out on their journey
and Flyaway was going too.*

Now that the mother bee did not have to fly out of doors for the food, she laid eggs and eggs and still more eggs, so that the nursery was full of baby sisters of all sizes, from the egg to the cocoon age. As soon as the older ones came out of their cocoons, and had eaten and grown strong, they helped care for the growing babies. If they did not fly off to bring home fresh food, they stayed with their mother to help her with the nursery work.

So the happy, busy Old Bumble and the daughters spent the days, doing together all the hard though pleasant tasks of bringing up a large family of children. Each day seemed much like another, and each new sister that crept out of her cocoon looked like her oldest sisters, only some were larger. Not one was as big as Old Bumble, though. Not one!

Much of their work was flying from flower to flower for nectar to make honey out of, and to gather pollen to take home in the baskets on their legs. And while they were doing this for themselves and their younger sisters, they carried pollen from flower to flower, which helped make the seeds grow. So we can have the big red clovers and many other flowers they visit, so long as we do not destroy the bumblebees.

Time passed in this way until about the first of August. Then something different came to pass in this wonderful home. Some sisters crept out of their cocoons, who were as big as their mother—every bit as big as Old Bumble! And what is more, about the same time, some brother bees crept out of their cocoons: the very first brothers that Buzz and Hum and Flyaway ever had—Old Bumble's very first sons!

These brothers did nothing to help their sisters who had tended them while they were growing up. These sons of the family did nothing to help their mother. But the sisters and their mother could do for themselves and each other, so it made little difference to them what the gay bumblebee lads did if they kept out of the way. And they did this for the most part, having a fine time of it, flying from flower to flower, eating as much as they liked, but taking nothing home for the others.

And those August sisters, those big ones who looked like their mother—what did they, who were strongest of all, do in the home where they had grown up? Well, they sipped at the honey-mugs their smaller, older sisters had filled; and then, when they were strong, they sipped again. Some went to flowers, too; but some went only to the mugs in the nursery. They drank long, until their honey-sacks were filled. They needed food to last a long, long time, as a camel needs water enough to last him during a whole trip across the desert. It was their good-bye feast, and when it was done they went out through the doorway of that wonderful nursery. And they never came back again.

Never!

They flew about a little while, and then, when they were ready, they crept into their bedrooms, each one by herself, and fell into their August doze.

Ah me, the lazy things! There was clover yet, and many a sweet flower that needed its pollen carried for it, that it might have seeds. The smaller sisters, not nearly so strong, were still cheerfully at work, though their wings were tattered and torn and their fine fur coats were ragged. And these so fresh and big, with whole wings and new coats, weren't they ashamed to sleep the summer days away?

No, they were not ashamed. It was not for them to tear their wings and spoil their clothes. Not yet! They had nothing to do in the world but to rest and save their strength. That is what their mother did the year before.

So we will not call them lazy any more even if they did sleep so long. They rested while the hot August sun shone over the earth, and kept it all so warm that they did not sleep soundly, but moved now and then, as if they were dozing before a fire and just taking naps.

They rested while the red and yellow leaves fell to the ground like a gay and beautiful shower! They rested while the snow followed after the leaves, and the cold made them numb in their beds.

It was time enough to be up and doing when Spring called again. And shall we hope that when they wakened, brave and beautiful as their mother had been the year before—shall we hope that, when they flew low, humming their happy hunting song, the children of men had left spring flowers enough for the children of Old Bumble?

The strange house of Cecid Cido Domy.

CHAPTER III

THE STRANGE HOUSE
OF CECID CIDO DOMY

CECID CIDO DOMY may not have been a witch, though she had a name that sounded as if she might have been one; and if she did not bewitch that willow branch, just what did she do to it? For, to begin with, the branch was just like any of the others on the willow; and by the time Cecid Cido Domy got through with it, it changed into a cone, shaped much like those that grow on Christmas trees.

In fact, it changed before she got through with it, and there she was now right in the very middle of the very middle room. For the cone was a house with many rooms in it, though she herself never went outside the middle one—that is, she never did until she left Willow House for good.

There were strange doings in Willow House, too—much to interest anyone, with guests who came by day and by night and visitors who lived there just as if it was their house instead of Cecid Cido Domy's.

One night a tiny creature came and found Willow

House in the dark. She was dressed in soft gray, and when she was not flying, her wings folded down about her something like a long cape. The inner ones were gray as ashes, and the outer ones were darker gray, with bright brown upon them that was almost red; and they all had gray fringe that was softer and prettier than any other trimming could have been. She did not even knock, but she left an egg in one of the rooms, and her daughter, when she hatched out, lived right there, eating all the food she wanted and having a happy time in the shelter someone else had made ready, with no trouble at all to herself.

Once another caller came in the day-time and left her egg in another room. She had no colors on her wings, and you could see right through them. The hind ones were fastened to the front ones by little hooks, so she looked as if she had only two wings when she really had four. She was a relative of a wasp, but she was not a wasp; and instead of a sting she carried a little saw. That is why people called her Sawfly. Her saw was a sort of tool she used when she was laying her egg, so that she could get it in far enough where it would be safe. Well, her daughter hatched out and made herself at home and ate all she wanted, just as the daughter of the gray moth had done.

Neither of these was any relation to Cecid, but the next guest was a sort of cousin. She made herself very much at home indeed, and left more than one egg at Willow House. She wasn't half as big as a mosquito, so of course her eggs were not large enough to take up much room. Her children, when they hatched, looked like Cecid, only they were even tinier; but they never went into the middle room, and as she did not go out, these cousins grew up in the same house without ever meeting each other.

There were other guests, too, though none of them were invited to come. But it was all the same to Cecid Cido Domy. Guests might come and guests might stay or go! So long as they did not enter her middle room, or eat the food she needed for herself, or tear the house down too much, she was neither sorry nor glad. Indeed, she did not even know what went on in this wonderful house of hers.

And her house was pretty, too, as well as wonderful. It was shaped, as you know, very much like the cones that grow on Christmas trees; but the color was different. The shingles were soft and fuzzy and curved up about it like the petals of a rosebud, so that they were up-end-down and not the way houses are usually shingled. But you must remember that this was the house of Cecid Cido Domy, and not be surprised at anything about it. Or perhaps everything about it will surprise you, for it was all so queer and different from other houses.

How Cecid's house would look if it were cut in two.

It may have looked as much like a rosebud as it did like a cone; for the shingles were stained creamy white at the small end, and were touched with pink across the middle, while the wide-curved outside end was silvery

31

green. There never were prettier shingles made; and to think that, if it had not been for Cecid Cido Domy, each of them would have been just a green willow leaf!

The way she changed green leaves into fuzzy shingles is a secret. Some people think that she poured out a juice on the tip of the twig in the spring, when the leaf-buds were ready to grow very fast, and that this juice had power to change the way they grew. All we really know about it for sure is that, whenever Cecid Cido Domy lives on a willow branch, a wonderful house grows up around her, and that the house is made of what started to be just green willow leaves.

The middle room had bare wooden walls, with the tiny brown boards going straight up and down. They met at the top in a point, but were not fastened together. That was the door to the room, and as Cecid stayed in and the other wee people in the house stayed out, this door was not used often. In fact, it was used but once, and that was the time Cecid Cido Domy went out never to come back again.

But she had not yet left home, for the March winds were blowing and it was not warm enough. The pussies on the next willow bush had crept out of their little brown winter covers and looked as if they were sleeping in the sun. Some little birds with black caps on their heads were flying quickly here and there, and were so happy that they sang "Chick-dee-dee, dee-dee," and then called "Fee-bee" sweetly, in a different tone, as if one song were not enough to show how joyous they were.

All this meant nothing at all to Cecid Cido Domy, who slept in her wooden room, as she had done ever since she went to sleep the fall before when cold weather came on.

She was not much to look at when she went to sleep— only a little wiggly thing so short that it would have taken eight of her to be an inch long. She had no feet, and from her shape it was hard to tell which end her mouth was on. She had nothing that looked like a head, and one end seemed about as much like a tail as the other. The easiest way to tell which was which, was to see what end she stood on; for she

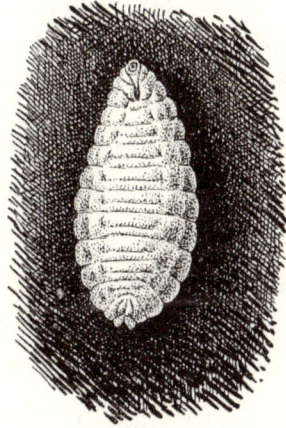

She was not much to look at when she went to sleep.

stood on her tail and not on her head. Either she was yellow at one time and pink at another, or she was a color that looked different to different people; for some called her yellow and some called her pink.

No, she was not much to look at, being so small and having so little shape. But you can't always tell, from just looks, how much any living thing can do; and Cecid Cido Domy was wonderful if she didn't look it—wonderful enough to get a home for herself and others, too, by making a willow-switch blossom into a rose.

She did another wonderful thing, too, before she

went to sleep in the fall. That was after she had taken the last meal she was ever to have in Willow House, and after she had changed her dress a few times, and was as long as one eighth of an inch. She was old to be so tiny, for she had hatched out in the spring, and it had taken her until fall to grow even as big as that, though her house had grown up about her quite quickly.

The wonderful thing she did before she went to sleep for the winter was to spin a little box all about herself. It was not a warm one, for it was so thin it could be torn by the slightest touch. But there was nothing in the middle room to tear it except Cecid, and you may be sure she didn't, after working so busily to make it.

Although she did not have enough of a mouth to make her head look like a head, it was as much as she needed, and it had a hole opening into it out of which she could spill a sort of silk glue—the thinnest, finest glue you can imagine. As soon as it touched the air it grew stiff so that it did not stick to her. In this way she made a little thin box all about her, somewhat as a caterpillar spins a silk cocoon. It was the color of water, so that she could be seen inside the box, as if it had been glass.

There Cecid Cido Domy slept, standing on her tail, in her glassy silk box in the middle room of Willow House.

While she slept a change came to her as strange as the change which came to the willow when the tip of one of its branches turned into a rosebud cone. She changed from a maggot, with both ends pointed

34

and looking much alike, into a tiny pink pupa, with something on her sides that looked the way wings do when they begin to grow.

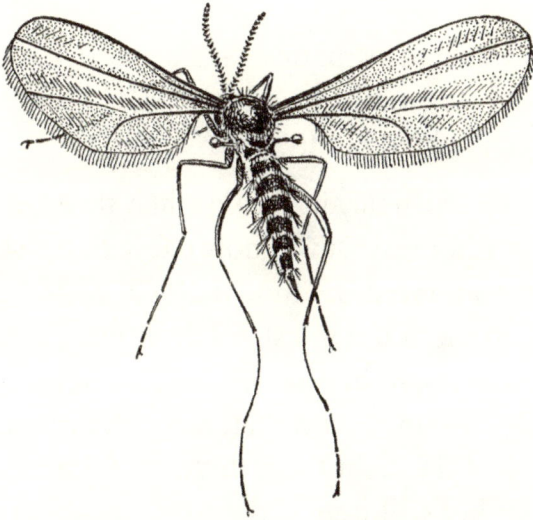

Then she changed into a little midget.

Then she changed from a pupa into a little midget that looked something like a small-sized mosquito. By this time she was awake, and had pushed her way out of her glassy box and up, up through the middle of the middle room to the doorway where, for the very first time in her life, she stood where it was light. She was no longer in the dark, and she was no longer blind. Eyes had come to her in her great change, and she now had a good little head to wear them on and two long feelers to wave out in front. She did not stand on her tail any more, and she had six slender legs to hold her up and walk on. But she did not need just to walk, for she had wings. There was something strange about them, though, for she had but two.

Now Van and Bumble and Jack and Carol all had four wings; and could Cecid Cido Domy get along with two?

Well, she had as many as a mosquito has, and two are enough for a bird or a bat! Besides, she had two pegs which helped her fly.

It was a warm day in spring when she stood by the door of her home, that was now old with the storms of winter. It was about the time that willow-leaves begin to grow. So she could not stand there long, for she had an errand to do in the world. A very important errand it was, too. So important that, if she did not attend to it and at just the right time, there would be no willow houses for her children, and it would be a pity to have them hatch too late for that.

Off she went—her two wings and two pegs were enough, and it would never, never do to be too late! And here and there, near the bank of a little river, Cecid Cido Domy might have been seen that spring, seeking the willow-tips and laying her eggs one by one so that her little blind, legless babies might hatch when each willow-switch was just ready to have its leaves turned into shingles, stained creamy white and pink and silvery green, and curved like the pretty petals of a rosebud about the middle room, which should hide within its bare wooden walls a secret all its own.

And so, when the March wind blows the fur of the pussies sunning themselves on the willow-twig, and the happy bird with a black cap calls, "Chick-dee-dee,

dee-dee," and, perhaps more sweetly still, "Fee-bee," is it very strange that we pick some twigs that have no pussies on them, but, instead, a little sleeping insect in a glassy silk box in the heart of a fuzzy cone—hoping that we may see, when the days are warmer, the little creature come forth and shake her wings? For fairy or witch or what-not, Cecid Cido Domy is a wonder well worth seeing; and if she does not bewitch the willow-branch, just what does she do to it?

CHAPTER IV

POLY, THE EASTER BUTTERFLY

EASTER came in April that year, which was much earlier than Poly, who lived in the north, would have come out of her chrysalis if she had not put it where she did. The fall before, when she was ready to spin a peg for her tail to hang on and a belt to hold herself up with, while she waited to be a butterfly, she left the parsnip plant she had been living on in the garden and took a very hurried trip. It was the first time she had ever been away from her parsnip home, but now that she had started, she seemed to be in a rush to get away from it. At the same time she seemed to be trying to get somewhere else as quickly as she could. So while she was running away from one place and running into another, she climbed up the side of an empty house and crept in through a broken window. When she had gone as far as that, she settled down for the winter and turned into a chrysalis then and there—that is, she did so after she had spun a peg for her tail and a belt to hold her up.

Soon after that, Papil, another caterpillar from

another parsnip plant, traveled along much the same path that Poly had taken, and in much the same hurry to get away from somewhere and go somewhere else. He found the broken window, too, and went in and spun a tailpeg and a belt and changed into a chrysalis, just as Poly had done.

The house that they chose would have been as good as an old shed or a fence-post if it had stayed empty. But it didn't. When the Soldier came back from France, his head was so tired

Papil spun a peg and a belt and changed into a chrysalis just as Poly had done.

that he wanted to go to the home where he had lived when he was a little boy, until he was rested.

That is how it happened that he found Poly and Papil when he was mending the window. At first he thought he would take them out to the shed. But when he touched Poly, she wiggled a little as if she wanted to be let alone. When he saw what a nice silk peg she had made for her tail to hold on to, and what a fine belt she had drawn about her to keep her in place, he didn't wish to take her down. So he let them both stay for company, and put flowering plants in the window so that they could have sweet cups to drink from when they came to be butterflies.

Poly stayed in her chrysalis cell all winter, for it was not so warm by the window as nearer the fireplace. And then, one day in April, she pushed against her cell until the door opened and she came out through the crack.

She was a butterfly now, but her wings were not big enough to fly with. They were just four limp, floppy little flaps, hanging down her back. She had to cling with her six long slender black legs to keep from falling—her wings were of no use. Four little wings good for nothing at all!

But wait! As Poly clung to the thin wall of her winter cell, the wings were getting bigger! They were twice as big as at first and still growing! My, oh my, oh my! How they grew! Do you suppose they were getting big enough to carry Poly to the blossoms?

Yes, and it was Easter Day. There were tall white lilies and little blue lilies and other flowers, too; and they were so sweet that Poly spread her wings when they were strong enough, and fluttered over to the little blue lilies, and uncoiled her long black tongue and drank, for she was thirsty.

And there, drinking nectar from the next lily, was Papil, who had come out that very same day and had found the pretty sweet cups first. So in the large bay-window, full of flowers, Poly and Papil spent their Easter Day together, and, though they did not know it, the Soldier watched them a long while and smiled.

When they become butterflies they drink
nectar from flowers.

Butterflies among the flowers are beautiful on any day, but at Easter time they have a special meaning.

There is a reason why people paint downy chickens on their Easter cards and give their friends lilies at that time. The live chick comes from the still egg; the live lily grows from the dull brown bulb. Such things make us think how wonderful life is.

So does the butterfly, who breaks the walls of the quiet chrysalis and comes out so full of life and beauty. Many years ago people loved the butterfly because of this, and gave her a sweet old name, "Psyche," which means "the soul."

It is no wonder that the Soldier smiled, with both lilies and butterflies to make life look beautiful to him that Easter Day.

Poly and Papil lived among the flowers for several weeks before Poly seemed to notice that there was a big pot of carrots and one of parsnips and one of celery growing there in the bay-window. These plants had no flowers, and why should Poly care about just leaves? She could not eat them if she tried, with her long tongue.

Ah, but there was a time when Poly had no long tongue—no tongue at all, in fact, for it was when she was only an egg; and in those days she had lived on the tip of a parsnip leaf. So we must not be surprised to find her, when she had eggs of her own, putting them on such leaves as she herself could have eaten when she was a caterpillar just hatched from an egg.

Now Poly in her caterpillar days could have eaten

If you find a caterpillar like Poly,
she can teach you a great deal.

a great many kinds of leaves besides parsnips, if her mother had left her on them; but I have never heard that she could eat anything that did not belong to the parsnip family. So if you find a caterpillar like Poly eating any sort of leaf, you may nod your head wisely and say, "That belongs to the parsnip family," whether you ever saw that kind of plant before or not. You see that, if you know a Poly caterpillar, she can teach you a great deal about plants. She never makes a mistake. Why, she would even go so far as to starve to death if any one tried to feed her a leaf that belonged to the wrong family. That is, when she is a caterpillar. When she is a butterfly, she drinks nectar from blossoms of many families and carries pollen for them all. But when egg-laying time comes, she flies back to the parsnip family just as if she remembered something.

Now some of the plants in this family are kinds that men, as well as Hexapods, like to eat, and we grow them for food. That is the reason we sometimes have to keep Poly's children out of our gardens, if there are so many of them that they eat more than we think we can spare. It is not hard to keep them out, for they do not hide and are easily seen. Some people let them have a few plants at the end of the row, because they like to watch the funny caterpillars, and because they love to see the beautiful butterflies they change into. That is what the Soldier did.

Zene, who hatched out of Poly's first egg, was contented enough when she crept from her shell on the tip of a celery-leaf. She hardly stopped to turn round before she began her green breakfast. Being a healthy baby, she was hungry, and ate most of the time except when she had to change her dress. This she did for herself from the very first, for Poly never did anything for her children after she had put her eggs on the right plants. She had taken care of her own dresses when she was a caterpillar, and if her daughter couldn't do the same, so much the worse for Zene!

But Zene could! Of course she could! Only it was hard to do, and it made her so nearly sick every time she changed her dress that for two days she couldn't eat a thing. She just spun a thin mat of silk and rested on that. You might think that Zene would have gone on wearing the same one if it was so much trouble to change.

Maybe she would, if she could. But she was such a hungry little thing that she grew larger than her dress, and her head got bigger than her skull, and grew out of it at the back, until it looked like a bunch inside the neck of her tight old dress. Of course, when she got as fat as that, there was nothing to do but push and jerk until she broke something. The first thing that ripped was a seam right around her collar, and of course when that tore—off dropped her skull!

That gave her new head a chance to come out of the collar-hole, and then she crept right out after her head. And there was her old dress lying empty on the leaf.

Zene had a funny habit. Almost every time she changed her dress, she turned round after she had crept out of it and ate it up before she went on with her celery salad. It tasted good to her, so she did not waste it. When she didn't need it outside any more, she put it inside. She didn't eat her skull. That just rolled off the leaf.

Each dress lasted about a week before she had to change, and each new one was prettier than the one before. Her first ones had little bunches on them and a wide white sash shaped something like a saddle. They did well enough, but you ought to have seen her last dress. That was lovely! It was a pretty shade of green, with black bands for trimming, and every black band had a row of yellow spots on it.

It was a showy dress, Zene's last one. It could be seen nearly as far as anyone could see the celery plant she lived on, and she never tried to hide. Even after the weather grew warm, and the Soldier put her out of doors, she didn't.

Now when you come to think about it, that seems queer. When Van was chased, she hid by making herself look like the bark on a tree. Carol sat still in the sand and didn't show. Jack had two ways of hiding, both good ones. Perhaps Ann Gusti's funny trick was the best of all, though Gryl did very well, as you would find out if you ever tried to catch him for a pet.

But Zene! There she stayed right on the upper side of the leaf and way out on the edge, no matter who came along.

Now, when an animal, whether it has four feet or more, does not hide itself when things come near it, there is some very good reason.

Do you know what a wood-pussy is? That pretty animal, with black and white stripes and a tail like a plume, walks slowly and unafraid along the path. You can see him when he is still far off. If you wish to walk the other way, you have plenty of time. If you choose to go and meet him, he does not bother to turn out to the right to let you pass. He has shown you his black and white stripes as a warning. If after that you are foolish enough to come too near—you will wish you hadn't, that is all. The wood-pussy does not care. He doesn't mind the way he smells.

Now, can it be that Zene was unafraid during all her caterpillar days? Did nothing scare her? Did Daddy Bird try to take her home to his young ones? Was the white sash on her baby dresses to show where she was? Were the black and green stripes on her last pretty dress a warning?

Well, something shook the leaf she was on one day, sharply and quickly, and this is what happened:

Zene threw up her head, and just behind it, from a slit in her back, she pushed out a pair of soft orange-colored horns. And just then there was a queer, oh, a very queer and very strong smell all around that celery plant.

I think it would have made you laugh if you had seen her. The Soldier laughed, and said something about a "gas-attack"; but that is soldier talk, and perhaps you will not understand what he meant.

Zene's pair of horns was something like a pocket with two long pointed corners turned inside-out. In a moment she drew it down behind her head so that it was right-side-out, inside her body, and all out of sight; and the strange smell was soon gone.

But though it could not be seen, the horn-pocket was there just the same, and already filled again with gas or whatever it was that Zene poured into the air when she threw her orange-colored pocket inside out and showed her horns. The stuff in her pocket is sour, and burns if it touches the tongue. Maybe Daddy Bird would not like that. So maybe Zene's bright stripes were one warning, and maybe the smell was another.

Perhaps her pretty dress, that could be seen so far, was like a danger-flag, and was a signal to other little creatures not to come too near her if they didn't like queer smells and sour, burny tastes.

However that may be, it is certain that Zene never seemed scared, and never hid from anything until she was ready to throw away her last dress, pocket and all.

When that time came, she left her celery plant in a hurry, and went somewhere else as fast as she could. She climbed up the side of the house near where Poly had the fall before, but didn't go in through the window. That was mended. Instead, she prepared to hide on the outside of the house right in plain sight.

First she rested for a whole day with her head pointed straight up and her tail pointed straight down. Once in a while she would swing a few loops of silk by moving her head, but not often. The second day she turned around so that her head was down and her tail was up. Then she went to work and spun silk from a tube that opened in her mouth. She swung out a silk thread as far as her head would reach to one side without moving the rest of her body. Then she grabbed the thread with her first pair of feet, which seemed more like arms, and pulled it back something as a man hauls up a rope "hand over hand." That made little folds in it, and she stuck the folded silk thread to the board with silk glue. Then she swung out her head to the other side, and pulled back the thread with her "hands," and glued down that folded part. This was the way she made her peg of silk, swinging her head from side to side and pulling back each thread in folds and sticking it down. It was a firm peg and a little curved, and it took her about half an hour to make it.

As soon as it was done, she turned round again so that she was head up and tail down once more. Her tail seemed to be in a hurry to find the peg, and felt around for it as if it were hunting for something. After lifting her tail up and feeling to one side and then the other, she at last hit the peg, and then she took right hold of it with the hooks in her last pair of feet and tangled them up in the silk threads and pulled tight until she held fast. She had hitched herself by her own tail and couldn't get away.

But she was not yet ready to be a chrysalis. For Zene was not going to hang head down like Van while she waited to be a butterfly. No, she was going to sleep head up, so she needed more than a tail-peg to hold her.

What she needed was a loose belt reaching from the board around her body. So she spun it. She glued the end of the first silk to the side of the house, and then spun a loop in front of her, stretching it up between her first and second pairs of legs, using the first pair like arms to catch it into place when she had spun it long enough so that her head could bend down and fasten the other end to the house. Thus she spun her belt, holding it up something like a skein of yarn in her "arms," and gluing the end to the board each time.

Once it broke while it was still very weak, and she fell way over to one side. But brave patient little Zene, with her tail hitched fast, felt her way back into place and began all over again.

After about half an hour's hard work on the belt that, too, was done, and Zene drew down her head and stuck it up inside the belt, and there she was fastened, tail down and head up, for her sleep.

Two days later she began to stretch and jerk inside her striped dress. What happened then was funny and wonderful.

Zene's dress ripped a little way down the middle of the back just behind her head, and something shaped like a little pug-nose stuck out. Then two little things like ears pushed up and split her skull and knocked it off. Then the queer thing inside Zene's dress, that had the pug nose and the ears, pushed the dress down toward the tail like a little wad of clothes it was going to step out of. Then it jerked its tail out of the clothes and poked it out over them and caught its tip into the tail-peg again and wiggled, and then the dress dropped to the ground.

And was that really Zene, with a funny pug-nose and two funny ears? It didn't look anything like Zene while she was a caterpillar, and it certainly didn't look as Zene would when it came time for her to be a butterfly.

But Zene was inside that queer-shaped little case, for all that. And at last she had hidden; for the case soon grew to be about the color of the board on the side of the old house, and she could not be seen far away.

Zene did not sleep all winter like her mother in the chrysalis case, but changed into a butterfly in about two weeks, and laid her eggs on some caraway leaves.

It was still summer when her children hatched, and Poly, the oldest and named for her grandmother, did all the things her grandmother had done except getting inside the Soldier's house to make her chrysalis. It was late in May when she wakened in the spring. But as butterflies have their own calendars instead of ours, perhaps it was her Easter Day, just the same.

When you stop to think about it, you remember
that a bitter-sweet vine does not have thorns.

CHAPTER V

JUMPING JACK

You would never have thought, to see Jack, that he could jump. He looked as if he had grown on the bitter-sweet vine. He looked like a thorn that would stay there even in winter, like the bright red berries.

But when you stopped to think about it, you would remember that a bitter-sweet vine does not have thorns—not real ones. Then you would point your finger at Jack and say, "You can't fool me, sir! You are not a thorn"; and before you got through telling him that, Jack would be gone.

He wouldn't jump, though. Not that time! He would just slip around to the other side of the branch, where you could not see him, and sit there looking as if he had not moved, and as if that were the place he had always grown in. So you would play hide-and-seek with him for a long time: Jack would hide and you would seek. But if Jack is touched too hard, then he is nimble and he is quick and he will jump off with a snap and spread his four wings and fly a little way.

For Jack can fly, and so can Jill, his little mate; but

they will both come back again to drink the sap of the bitter-sweet vine.

There they sit now, with their sharp slender beaks stuck right down through the bark, and drawing the juice up through the hollow tube, as you suck lemonade through a straw. They find it pleasant to sit there all the summer day and sip the juice of the vine.

Do you think Jack and Jill look like little birds? Well, that is just what a man who watched them nearly seventy years ago thought, too. Not that Jack and Jill are seventy years old. Oh my, no! But there were some others just like them on bitter-sweet then.

Our own little Jack and Jill hatched out of their eggs in May. They had stayed in their nests all winter without hatching. Just think of it! It didn't hurt them one bit. I don't know why; but it didn't. The nests they lived in while they were eggs were holes their mothers cut in the stem of the vine and tucked full of eggs in little rows. Jack had twelve brother- and sister-eggs in the nest with him, and Jill had even more.

Jack and Jill

Jack was the last egg his mother put through the

hole in the bark into the nest. When he was safely poked down at the end of the row, she covered the hole with something that looked like the nice sticky frosting that is dripped from a spoon to the top of a cake. It wasn't sweet, so it couldn't have been frosting; but that is the way it looked, and it was in a wavy heap almost as big as Jack's mother.

Now wasn't that a good way of tucking her eggs in—to plaster them down with a sticky white blanket? Jill's mother made her nest just the same way. So there they were, snug as could be, little Jack and Jill and all their brother- and sister-eggs.

Think of the things that were to happen before they could hatch! Ann Gusti was still playing her clown tricks in the meadow, with the big blue sky for a tent, several weeks after Jack and Jill were tucked into their beds. Gryl sat before his open door, and fiddled a happy lullaby of "Cri-cri-cri." Luna, brown as a nut, lay on the ground in her own silk bedroom, fast asleep, too.

Cold weather came, when the ice did not melt even in the daytime and when the chilly earth was wrapped in a deep blanket of snow, as white as the cover Jack's mother had put over him and much thicker.

There were a few days in January when the snow thawed, and Van wakened in the hollow tree, and came out, and flew about the sunny places in the lane, and drank at the edge of a little pool.

Candlemas Day came, and Old Bumble was so sound asleep she never even buzzed.

And all this time Jack slept under his blanket, that was wrapped so closely to the twig that the snow could not sift in, and stuck down so tightly that the wind could not lift the corners.

Even when the willow pussies crept out along the twigs to warm their fur in the March sun—even then Jack was asleep.

Some pretty blue lilies blossomed for Easter Day, but Jack was still a tiny Easter egg himself, and it was not yet time for him to hatch.

And then at last May came and woke him. How did she call him when he had slept so long and so soundly? Perhaps with her sunshine, which brooded the nest of eggs in the bitter-sweet vine with its warmth, as a mother hen broods over her nest of eggs in the hay with her cozy feathers.

And here he was—a feeble baby, so wee you would need a magnifying glass to see him with! What was he to do with that heavy blanket over him? If his mother had stuck it down so tightly that even the strong north wind could not move it, how was Jack to get out of bed? Poor little Jack with his twelve brothers and sisters! Whatever were they to do?

Well, here he comes, like a tiny Jack-in-a-box, poking his head right up through the white blanket. He does not try to lift it; he just sticks up his yellow head and red eyes, and pushes himself out of bed.

Of course Jack is thirsty, and of course a baby who can get out of his nest all by himself the first day can feed himself, too. So out he creeps to the tender leaf, and digs his little beak down into it, and takes his first drink of sap.

He likes it! Oh my! my! how he likes it! He likes it so well that for seven whole days he hardly stops drinking.

By that time his first baby clothes are so tight that he can not swallow another drop. What is the greedy youngster to do about that? His clothes are grown on him, too! Think of it!

Never mind. Baby Jack is so strong now, after taking a drink that is seven days long, that all he has to do is to stretch himself; and this rips his clothes in a little seam near the back of his head and tears his baby cap. Now he can pull his head out of the old cap and then get out of his first baby clothes through the torn place.

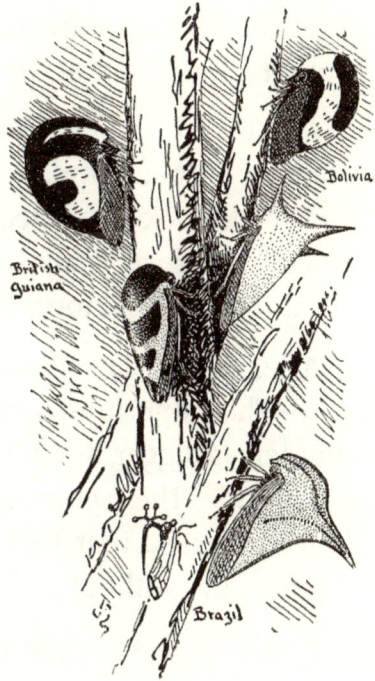

Jack's foreign cousins.

His first dress had long hairs on it, but his second one, which grew on him under the old one, does not have these hairs. Instead, it has six lumps in a row on the middle of his back. You would think that the second dress, growing under the first one, would be even smaller and tighter.

But as it stretches as Jack grows, he can take another long drink before his second dress is stretched as big as it can be. So he puts down his beak again and drinks for six more days. Then he needs a third dress, which he gets in just the same way as before—he creeps out through a torn place at the back.

This time he still has the six lumps in a row in the middle of his back, and, besides, a hump has begun to grow at the back of his head. While he looks like that, he takes his third drink of bitter-sweet sap, and this lasts about six days, too.

After that he gets his fourth suit of clothes—much like the third one, lumps and all; only the hump on his shoulders is bigger, and there are two little flaps below on each side. These clothes keep on stretching for two whole weeks, so that Jack has a chance to drink for fourteen days without stopping for his next dress.

But dear, dear! when he creeps out of his fourth dress, what a hump he does have! It has grown way up over his head. Yes, Jack is a hump-back, and all the doctors in the world can not cure him. And the two flaps on each side are much, much bigger.

Well, never mind! The six lumps down the middle of his back and the hump on his shoulders and the flaps on his sides do not bother him a bit. He is as healthy and as thirsty as ever. By this time he is strong enough to dig his beak right down into the stem of the vine, where the sap is running freely. All his clothes are pale at first, but grow darker as they get older, when they are gray or brown, and trimmed with red and sometimes with a little white.

Jack sits and sips and grows in his fifth dress just as he did in all the other four; and at last this one becomes too tight just as the others did, one after another. That does no harm, for he can still have one more suit of clothes. So when these get too tight, he stretches and stretches inside of them, until they rip open and he can crawl out.

When he is all out and has rested a bit, he puts his beak down into the bitter-sweet vine and goes on drinking as if nothing much had happened.

Why Jack, don't you know that a wonderful change has come to you? Don't you know that the hump on your shoulders is so big that it makes you almost twice as tall as you would be without it? Don't you know that four of your legs now look something like tiny leaves? Don't you know that your two hind legs are longer than they were before, and that you can jump? Oh, how nimble and quick you can be when you jump! And don't you know, you funny Jack, oh, don't you know that the flaps on your sides have changed into wings and that you can fly away and back again? Don't you know—don't you even know that you are no longer a growing baby but a grown-up treehopper?

No matter how much you may drink now, you cannot be any bigger, for this is the last suit of clothes you can ever have—the very, very last!

How much of all this do you suppose the queer little

chap really understands, as he sits on the vine looking like a thorn?

Well, just as much as Jill knows, who hatched on a May day, too, and grew up in the very same way, humped back and all.

But while Jack can only sit and sip and jump and fly and play hide-and-seek with you as the summer days go by, Jill finds something else to do before the weather gets cold.

Jill has a neat little tool at the end of her body, and it would be a pity not to use it. For one thing, it is a cunning knife, and with it she cuts a hole in the twig and digs out a nest for her eggs. For another thing, it is a sort of bubble-blower, and with it she stirs up her foam that looks like frosting. And last, it is a little spoon that she uses to drip the pretty white sticky stuff down over the nest of eggs. Slowly, back and forth and down under and up over, she moves her spoon, standing all the time on tiptoe to make the wavy rows of foam so very, very carefully.

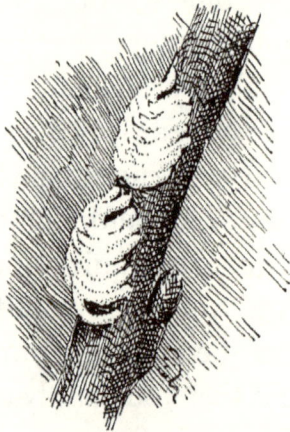

This is the foam that stiffens into a blanket to cover her eggs.

For this is the foam that stiffens into a blanket to cover her eggs; and as she can not stay on the cold twig to take care of them through the winter days that will be coming, she must do what she can to make the blanket just right.

She makes a good one, little Jill does: one so like the one that her mother put over her and the one that Jack's mother put over him when they were eggs in a nest, themselves, that you could not tell which of the three was the best.

So there they will stay, tucked in snug and safe. Jack Frost will be about when the cold nights come, but he will not harm them. North Wind will whistle through the bitter-sweet vine and shake the red berries, but he can not lift the blanket Jill stuck down. And many other strange and wonderful things will happen during the days of fall and winter and early spring.

But, after all, nothing will be stranger and more wonderful than when May calls Jill's babies, and each little yellow head with bright red eyes comes popping up through the white fluff like a Jack-in-a-box.

A May day is a pleasant time, when things like that are happening out on the bitter-sweet vine!

CHAPTER VI

NATA, THE NYMPH

ONCE upon a time Nata could not walk or fly or swim. Of course that was when she was an egg.

While she was a helpless little thing like that, her mother dropped her into the water and flew off and left her.

This sounds cruel, and when you know that Nata's mother was the creature that people sometimes call the devil's darning-needle, and that children sometimes talk about, with scared looks on their faces, when they say that she will sew up their lips and maybe their eyes and ears, too, if she catches them—when you know that was Nata's mother, maybe you will think she was just wicked enough to let Nata drown.

But it is always the best way not to be quick to believe bad things about anybody, because most of the time they are not true. That is how it was with Nata's mother. She never tried to catch a girl or boy in her life and she wasn't anybody's darning-needle, and she couldn't sew up anything even if you held her right up to it.

And Nata did not drown. She hatched out as well in the water as Lampy did in the ground, or as Luna did on a green oak leaf. It was just the right place for her, and her mother had done her no harm in putting her there.

In fact, Nata's mother is known to have done much good in the world—she caught so many flies and mosquitoes that she was sometimes spoken of as a mosquito hawk. She was a great hunter all her days, and her real name, after she got her wings, was Dragonfly.

When Nata hatched she had no wings and she was called a nymph, which was just a name she had while she lived in the water—the same as Poly was called a caterpillar while she was living on a parsnip plant.

Nata, the nymph, looked as much like a grown-up dragonfly as Poly, the caterpillar, looked like a butterfly. Maybe she looked a little bit more like one, for she had six legs from the first to the last, while Poly started out with sixteen and ended up with six. But it would take more than the same number of legs to make Nata, a nymph, look like her mother, a dragonfly. What she did look like, it would be hard to say. Perhaps, more than anything else, she just looked comical.

At first, of course, she was tiny, as all things are that hatch out of small-sized eggs. From time to time, as she grew, she had several different bathing-suits, each one larger than the one before. The first one did n' t have a sign of wings on it; but as she grew bigger and changed one bathing suit after another, the signs of wings began to come, and then to grow bigger with each new suit.

Not real wings, you know—just signs of them that are called wing-pads, and that look like four little flat flaps on her back.

When she got large enough for a change, a new suit grew under the one she had been wearing, and then the old one ripped far enough for her to step out of the tear. She did this under water, so you may think she must have been washed very clean all the time. But, you see, she waded around where it was muddy so much that it was hard to tell what was mud and what was Nata, the mud-covered nymph; just as it was hard to tell what was sand and what was Carol, the sand-colored locust. So some of the mud would have to be washed off before we could see that Nata was comical.

To begin with, she wore a mask which covered nearly all of her face, as far up as her feelers in front and as far as her eyes at the side. This mask was as big for her as one would be for you if you make one by holding your arms together in front of you, bent up from the elbow so that you can cover your mouth and nose with your hands. If you do that, you can throw your mask out in front of you so that your face shows, and then draw back again and cover it up. Nata's mask was hinged like that, so that she could throw it out quickly and pull it back. Most of the time it was folded up tightly over her big mouth. It kept the mud out when she dived down head-first.

It did something else, too. For Nata was a hunter, and her mask was a little trap she carried around with her all the time. She hunted in the water as her mother

Nata was a hunter.

hunted in the air, and as Lampy hunted in the ground; only when her mother and Lampy hunted, they went after things. Nata didn't have to. She sat still with her trap folded over her face, and when a wriggler (that is the name of a young mosquito before it has wings) or something like that came near, she would just throw out her trap and pull her food right up to her mouth. It was a pretty good trap; it never got out of order, and every new bathing suit had hitched to it a new mask that was of the same sort only bigger than the one before.

Her feelers were just above the edge of the mask, so that she could move them around in the water. They were slender, and the seven joints in them were all very short so that she could not feel very far.

When the top of her head showed, the two eyes stuck out round like those of a frog. This made her look very wide-awake indeed. But when the front and side of her head showed, her eyes were different from any other kind I have ever seen. They had wide stripes of pale green and narrow ones of dark purple, and the stripes were slanted. Now eyes with green and purple stripes are pretty—very pretty; but they are funny, too, and her queer eyes and her queer mask, both together, were what made Nata's head so comical.

If her head was a strange one, so was her tail, for that was where the breathing tube was.

Of course no little Hexapod ever breathes through his head. Not Van or Gryl or Old Bumble or any of them. Grown-up ones, by the time they have wings, breathe through a row of little holes on each side of their bodies.

Most baby Hexapods breathe the same way, but Nata, the nymph, was different. She had a breathing tube with an opening at the tip of her tail. So it was almost as if she had a mouth at each end of her body—one to eat with and one to breathe with.

You know that most animals that live in the water have gills to breathe with. Nata did, too, and her gills were on the inside of her breathing tube.

When you breathe, you have to get oxygen out of the air. When Nata breathed, she had to get some oxygen that was in the water. So she would draw the water into her tube as we draw air into our lungs, and then push it out again as we push out the air.

So now you can see why, when Nata used to dive down head-first, she left the tip of her tail up out of the mud where there was some water. If she had stayed tail down and head up, she would have smothered.

Nata liked diving and did a great deal of it. Sometimes she would stand on her head down deep in the mud for a long time. It seemed to be one of her ways of hiding.

When she hid another way, she would lie down in the mud and then kick with all six of her little feet until she scratched out a hole in the mud, and her body would sink down deeper and deeper until she would be all covered up except her eyes and the top of her trap at her head-end and her breathing hole at her tail-end. While she was hiding that way she was usually hunting.

Nat was Nata's mate.

The mud Nata played in and hunted in was at the bottom of a pool a little off at one side in Shanty Creek. Now, you can tell from this something about what part of the country she lived in, because if it had been in some other places the name would have been Shanty Stream or Shanty Brook.

Nata did not stay in the mud at the bottom of the pool all the time. Now and then, though not often, she would walk out near the edge where the water was not deep, and put the mouth of her breathing tube up into the air; and it would look as if she could breathe that way, too. And sometimes she would run about among the wet dead grass-stems and other rubbish in the water near the edge.

One day she did this after a heavy rain, when there was a flood that had filled a hollow next the pool she lived in. The water spilled over from the pool into the hollow, and Nata happened to walk into the hollow where there were some good things to hunt that had gone over with the water.

That did very well for a day or two, and Nata stayed. She stayed so long that the water went lower and lower, until it no longer spilled over from the pool into the hollow.

Now, the hollow was small, and it did not take her many days to trap all the good things there were in it. After that, of course, there was nothing for her to do but wait; for she did not know anything about going from the hollow up the dry bank and over into the pool again. She couldn't think things out like that. She had a brain in her little head, too, and a wonderful one it was; but it didn't help her back into the pool.

It could help her wait, though, and that is what she did. She waited for seven days, and nothing—not so much as one mosquito wriggler—got into her trap. And all this time the water was sinking lower and lower in the little hollow, until by the end of the week there was not more than a cupful left. Then it rained until there was as much as would fill a dishpan.

Nata still waited, with her trap held up closed about her hungry mouth, for days and days and nights and nights, until another week went by, and she had nothing to eat even then.

By that time the water was gone from the hollow. There wasn't enough left to fill a thimble!

The dirt at the bottom was still soft and wet, though, and there Nata stayed, all alone and very hungry.

Poor little Nata, waiting in the mud! Four days went by while she had just air to draw into her breathing tube, for all the water was gone. So there were four more days to add to the other fourteen without food!

And Nata still waited. Do you wonder how she lived so long? Perhaps it was partly because she didn't tire herself all out fretting. She waited quietly most of the time, and rested. Partly too, it was because she was strong and because she was a hunter, and very often hunters have to wait a long time between meals. But eighteen days was longer than usual, and unless something happened to get Nata back into her pool she would—Oh dear, oh dear! what would become of her?

But something did happen. It was rain! There was thunder and lightning with it, but Nata didn't mind that. And there was a flood—a nice big one that spilled the pool over into the hollow.

In a little while after that, Nata found her way back to her old hunting-ground in the mud at the bottom of the pool. Perhaps she felt the motion of things swimming about in the pool. Perhaps she smelled something that tempted her back. Perhaps she just went walking around and happened to get home again as she happened to get lost.

Well—She came out of Nata's bathing suit.

Whatever way it was, she had a good time all the rest of the days she was a nymph. She caught plenty of food in her trap—nice tender juicy food. She played in the mud, sometimes diving down in it head first, and sometimes kicking it out from under her so that the trap on her head was where she could use it as well as the opening of the breathing tube in her tail.

Then one day, right in the midst of all this fun of diving and wading and hunting—one day she stopped doing the things that she had done all her life, and walked up out of the water to the shore of the pool, and climbed a little way up the stem of a plant, and then pretty soon all there was left of Nata, the nymph, was an empty bathing suit, just her shape, clinging to the plant.

Nata the Nymph is no more. She has gone, leaving her water-clothes all whole and good except the opening at the back where she pulled herself out of them. They look as if they were left waiting for her to come and slip into them again.

When will she come back and live in her pool?

Ah, Nata can never do that. Look, and you will know why!

See—flying along the bank of Shanty Creek, a beautiful creature with four wonderful strong wings and with eyes that gleam like living jewels! Oh, now she has stopped and is resting in the sunshine near Nat.

Well—She came out of Nata's bathing suit. Do you think she will ever need it again?

CHAPTER VII

LAMPY'S FOURTH O' JULY

No one had ever given Lampy so much as a penny. He had never earned any money. He had never found any. Here it was the Fourth o' July, and he couldn't buy even one fire-cracker! Not any of his little gang of Will-o'-the-Wisps had fire-crackers either, so you might think that they were going to have a dull time of it that night.

For the Will-o'-the-Wisps had a habit, during the summer, of meeting every evening about the time the stars came out, and having a frolic together. They never did any harm in the world. If the policeman saw them darting about after the curfew rang, he just smiled and never thought of such a thing as sending them to bed.

Why, indeed, should Lampy go to bed by night? He rested all day, like a little owl. Of course it is all right for some folk to sleep while it is dark. Van and Poly and Jack and Nata and Carol are awake all day, and so they need to rest at night. They are made that way, just as chickadees and robins are. Some flowers are like that, too, and shut up their pretty eyes as soon as it grows dark.

73

But Lampy! My, no! Miss the night-time? Sleep while the Big Dipper in the sky whirled slowly around the steady North Star? Doze while the evening primrose opened its lovely yellow cups of nectar and filled the air with sweet smells? Nap while the new moon sailed the skies like a little boat?

Why, even the bat, the cunning flying mouse, came out to enjoy the night air. Gryl was fiddling merrily in the fields. Luna was floating, like a fairy robed in white and green, through the woodland.

Oh, no! Lampy could not miss the night. Not that he listened to Gryl's music, or smelled the evening primrose, or watched the beautiful Luna, or even looked at the sky! But the night was good to him even without these joys. He was a part of it, and, besides, the whole gang of Will-o'-the-Wisps would be out for a Fourth-o'-July dance.

And the dance, just think of it, the dance was going to be in the air!

A Fourth-o'-July dance without fireworks, though—dearie, dearie, me!

Oho! Here was Lampy! He had crept out of bed at dusk, had lifted his upper wings, which covered the ones he used for flying, had shaken the wrinkles out of his thin under ones, and here he was, ready for the dance. And here was Jack-o'-Lantern, and here was Wah-wah-taysee, and here were Tinker Bell and Star-Light and Eye-Bright and Ray and Beam and Flash and Gleam—here were, indeed, the whole gang of Will-o'-the-Wisps! And every one of them carried a candle.

Over the marsh the mist is white,
The owl is calling through the night;
While, like a flock of dancing stars,
The Will-o'-the-Wisps are taking flight.

It was a dance to be happy about, for there was a time when none of these Will-o'-the-Wisps had any wings; and, as their six little tiptoes were not made for dancing, they had kept very close to the ground. So close, indeed, that they had lived right in it all the while they were growing up.

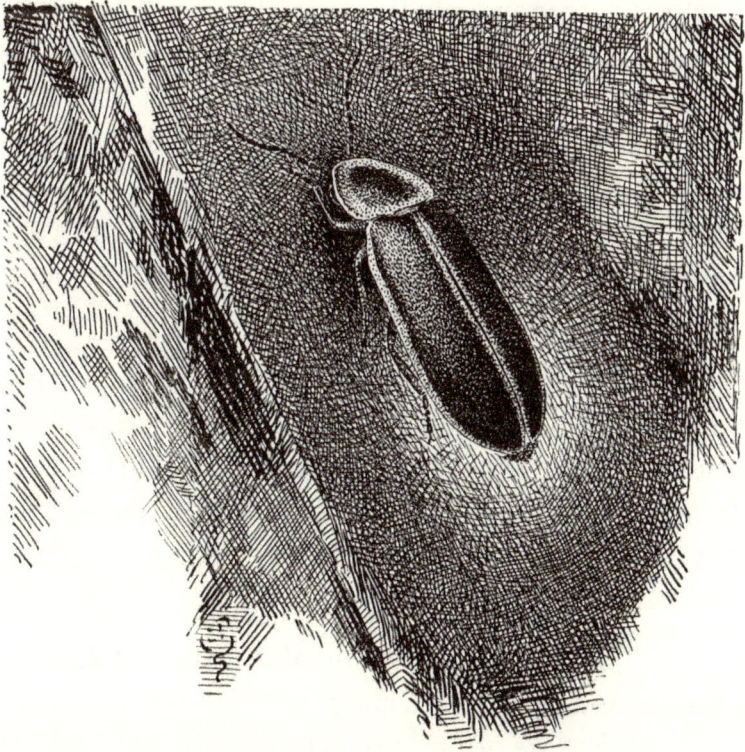

Oho! Here was Lampy.

75

No, Lampy had not always been flying through the air at night and resting wherever he happened to be by day. He had stayed where his mother had put him.

His mother, whose name was Firefly, wore over her head something that looked like a flat red-and-black hat, and her eyes were hidden under the broad yellow brim. She had a candle very much like Lampy's, only not quite the same in shape; and her wings were dark, with a light yellow edge all round. Like Lampy, she had rested by day, and had flown with her kind at night.

Her candle, it is thought, was a signal to other firefly beetles to come and join the dance, for they flew in large flocks near the swamps and over the low meadows. Her bright light did not give a steady glow like the North Star, but flashed and then went out and flashed again; as you can make a little pocket-light do by pressing it. So she could give "wig-wag" signals to her friends; and, as it was night, of course a flashing candle was better than a flag.

It is thought, too, that her candle was a warning to the night birds. It showed them just where she was, and they needn't swallow her up if they didn't like the taste of fireflies; just as Poly's bright dress showed the day folk where she was, so that they need not meet her unless they wished to.

Well, Firefly did not spend all the time in dancing at night and in resting when it was day. She had some eggs to take care of, and no matter how they may have looked to others, they were as good as gold to her.

Like a flock of dancing stars,
the Will-o'-the-Wisps are taking flight.

She buried her treasure—Lampy and the other little eggs. So their cradles were right in the dirt.

That was a handy place to be in, as Lampy found when he hatched and crept out of the egg. For he was born a hunter, and had to catch every bit of his own food.

Underground there were as many little things that Lampy liked to eat as there are on top of the ground for Biddy and her chicks, when they go hunting, or in the air for Nata, when she is grown up and flies about, or in the water for her, when she is a nymph and hides at the bottom of the pond.

Food enough in the world for everybody, if everybody goes about getting it in the right way; and the right way for Lampy was hunting in the ground!

So he dug little holes wherever he went, and made little caves and crept through them, and hunted and hunted and hunted all the time he was growing up. There, too, underground in his own dark hole, he changed his clothes when they felt too tight.

He was a queer-looking little thing, with a small head, and then a lot of joints for the rest of his body that were very much alike, except that the tail one had a little tool on it, and the three nearest his head had each a pair of short legs.

But one day he stopped looking like that. This was after he slipped out of his last suit of jointed clothes and went to sleep as soon as they were off. For little Lampy had grown to the time when he was to hunt no more through holes in the ground. He was going to sleep, and then he was going to waken and have wings to fly with and a candle to flash in the night-air. Think of that!

So he slept in the earth, and his bed under him was good clean dirt, and his blanket over him was good clean dirt, too.

Then, when it was the right time in the summer, he climbed up out of the ground. And that evening he flew over the low meadow to the marsh. There he found Jack-o'-Lantern and Wah-wah-taysee and Tinker Bell and Star-Light and Eye-Bright and Ray and Beam and Flash and Gleam.

They all danced in the air with their wings; and their candles, twinkling in the dark, were more beautiful than any other lights that could be seen—except the stars.

Oh, is it, then, a fairy sprite
That frolics with the elves at night?
The Will-o'-the-Wisps, on dancing wings,
But wake the dark with their delight.

Way, way off over the city, the sky-rockets and other fireworks showed where a crowd of men were having their Fourth o' July, too; but, do you know, with all their money, they had not been able to buy anything so lovely as the dance of the Will-o'-the-Wisps over the marsh!

For Lampy's candle was a secret, and no man has ever been able to make one like it. Not in this country or way over on the other side of the world in China, or anywhere, has any man ever made a candle such as Lampy and the other Will-o'-the-Wisps carried that night as they danced in the air above the marsh.

The most wonderful thing about it was that it was a cool light. You know that you cannot put your hand into the flame in the fireplace without getting burned. The rays of the sun are warm even when they have come many miles to us. You know that the light from kerosene or alcohol is hot enough to cook your dinner with, if there is an oven over it.

But Lampy's candle was pure light, with no heat. It was ten times as good a light as electricity makes, and fifty times as good as gas; and it was so cool that it did not burn his wings when they were folded right over it. It did not even make the end of his body, where he carried it, one bit warmer than his head.

Think of a light like that for a hot summer night!

And every one of them carried a candle.

Think of Lampy, without a penny in the bank, owning a candle such as the richest man in the world cannot buy! Think of having a secret that the wisest man never has guessed!

Mind, I do not say that no one ever will find out the secret of Lampy's candle. Maybe you will yourself, when you are grown up. Who knows? Just because no man or woman ever has, there is no reason to say that no one ever can.

If you ever do learn how to make a pure light that is not hot or even warm, what will you do with it? Will you keep your secret all your days? Will you sell it and be very rich? Will you give it to poor people in hot cities, that they may have a light that is cool? Will you give it to the sick, who should not have a warm light near their heads while they read? Or will you take it as Lampy did, and dance in the night with your friends, making the dark earth beautiful with your candles as the dark sky is beautiful with stars? And will you sing as you go:—

> "The flowers of dusk are gleaming bright
> And give their sweetness to the night;
> While day-folk sleep the dark away,
> We dance by pretty candle-light!"

CHAPTER VIII

CAROL

HER real name was Carolina Grasshopper, but we will call her Carol for short.

Carol was sitting in the sandy path, so near the road that, when any one passed, she had to move out of the way. This did not matter at all, for one place in the sand was as good as another to Carol.

It was noon-time of the hottest day of the summer,

It was noon-time of the hottest day of the summer.

and the sun shone down on her back and head, and the sand she was sitting on was almost hot enough to hurt your hand. It was the sort of day, in fact, when a person, if he does not put a damp cloth under his hat, is likely to have a sunstroke.

But Carol did not even have a hat on.

As for leaving that hot sand and having a nice cool wade in the little brook that sang "Bip-po bap-po" down through the shady woods to the river not far away—why Carol would never have done such a thing in the world! Had her mother not sat in the sand by the side of the road one year ago; and had not her two grandmothers done the same thing two years ago? And had her father and her two grandfathers ever found any better place than sand in the sun on a hot summer day? What was good enough for them was good enough for her.

So there she sat, looking about the color of a tiny heap of sand, just as her mother and grandmother and great-grandmother and great-great-grandmother, and all the rest as far back as you can count, had sat and looked before her. You might say it was a habit of her family.

Now Carol had two little fans, tucked down, one on each side of her. They were pretty when they were spread out—dull soft black, with yellow borders.

I once knew a girl who made one the same size out of black and yellow tissue-paper for her Doll Jane, and it was as cunning a fan as you could wish to see at a doll party.

But Carol was not at a party, and she was not using her fans. She had them all folded neatly under their brown covers, which kept them from getting worn and torn. She never once fanned herself with either of them!

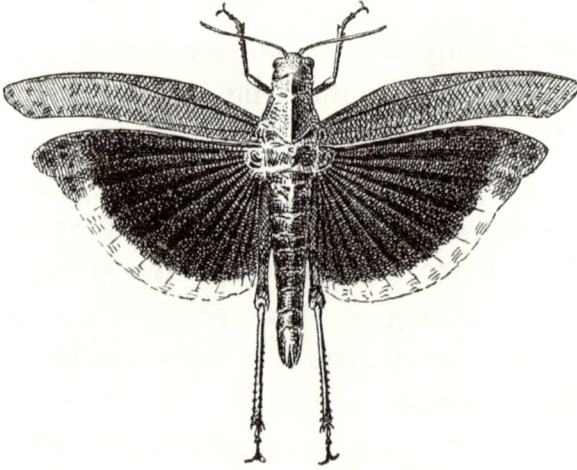

Now Carol had two little fans.

With these thin black-and-yellow dainty things tucked out of sight beneath the tough covers that made a sort of roof over her back, there was nothing to show where Carol sat. A little sand-colored grasshopper sitting on the sand—that was all.

Why, you could have stepped on her easily and never have known it! That is, you could, if she had not seen you coming; for Carol's eyes were very quick to see anything that moved toward her. If things stood still like trees, she did not bother about them. For nothing could catch her unless it came nearer and nearer and nearer. But if old Rover pattered down the road, or a bird flew close overhead and made a shadow, or a child ran by, then quick as a flash Carol would lift her fan-covers out of the way and spread her fans like little sails and fly off with them. For her black-and-yellow fans were wings!

And when you saw her fly away, perhaps you thought she was a butterfly. Maybe you thought she was a butterfly like Van, with dark wings and yellow borders. Maybe you were the little girl or boy who chased after her along the road, and looked right at her and didn't see her at all; for you were trying to find something with black-and-yellow wings, and Carol was just a sand-colored grasshopper sitting in the sand.

Well, if it was not you, it was some other girl and boy; and Carol led them half a mile along the roadside, fooling them time after time by showing them her broad wings in flight and then quickly hiding them under their covers, when she stopped to rest. And by-and-by the children grew so tired that they went off into the woods and found the brook, and waded there until they were cool.

On and on flew Carol, a little way at a time, now this way and now that, as dogs and children and horses and men sometimes came up the road and sometimes down. And once Carol was scared into the woods by a funny old cow with a crumpled horn, and the first thing she knew, she was sitting on some pretty leaves on the cool damp ground. But her brown sand-colored body showed very plainly on the green, and she didn't like the shady woods, and when she started for the

Perhaps you thought she was a butterfly.

roadside she bumped up against some bent grass-stems and fell down. Then she tried jumping out,—for two of her legs were big and strong for hopping; but she kept blundering against stems that were in the way. At last, she crept along more slowly without trying to fly or jump, and so got back to the roadside, where, although many things passed by, none could see her in the sand; and where, although she had often to hop and fly, there were no grass-stems above her to get tangled in.

But you mustn't laugh too much at little Carol, baking herself in the sunshine. If you had spent the winter where she did, perhaps it would take you all summer to get warm, too.

For Carol's mother—just think of it!—poked every egg she had down as far as she could reach into the ground, and poured over them a sort of froth that hardened about them. Carol herself was the very last egg her mother pushed down, so that she was on top of her brother and sister eggs, which lay under her in slanting rows. But even if she was on top, she had to stay there all winter long, and the ground froze as solid as a cake of ice, and part of the time the weather was colder than zero; and though the snow lay over her like a thick blanket, it was a cold bed for all that, and it is no wonder that Carol didn' t hatch for months and months.

When she did, poor little baby, she was buried alive under ground, and had a hard time of it pushing and pushing and pushing up; for she was the top of the brood and had to open up the way for her brothers and sisters as well as for herself.

But the world she found when she crept out of that hole was worth working to get into, for it was spring-time and the sun shone and there were some warm stones near by; and so Baby Carol hopped about and ate whatever she wanted, and was, so far as anyone could see, quite happy. All that, of course, was long before she could fly; for a grasshopper never has any wings until she is grown up, though every time she moults her brown skin, the little pads, that will some day be fans and fan-covers, grow bigger and bigger.

Yes, that was all many weeks ago, and Carol was now grown up and old enough to have a mate.

So we must not be surprised to see Carl Grasshopper talking pleasantly with her one day when they met on a large rocky place in the sun. But you may be surprised to know where he kept his voice, for though Carl had a throat and a mouth and lips, he used them to eat with and never spoke a word through them in his life. No, when Carl talked to Carol he did it by rubbing his great hind-legs against his sides; and this seemed to her the most natural way in all the world to be spoken to, for it was the way her father had talked to her mother. It was a gentle scraping sort of sound, and you would have to be near to notice it. But Carol was sitting on the same stone, and her ears, which she kept in as queer a place as Carl did his voice, could no doubt hear him very well.

Carl could sing, too, and his song was louder than his talking, and he had such a pretty way of doing it, that poets, who love pretty things, have sometimes sung about Carl's song in their verses. That makes a sort of double song, doesn't it?

When Carl wanted to sing, he would spring into the air about three feet, and hover almost in one place, with his wings spread and fluttering so fast that they made a clacking sound where the edge of the fans clicked against the edge of the covers.

And if poets have liked his song, is it strange if Carol was pleased?

But Carol could not spend all summer listening to music. She must hurry and get her eggs all buried before cold weather came. Carl did not help his mate dig a single hole; but you must not blame him for this, for his father had never dug a hole nor his grandfather nor his great-grandfather nor his great-great-grandfather, nor any father as far back as you can count. So you see it was not the fashion in Carl's family to dig holes for their mates to lay their eggs in.

And, after all, Carol had plenty of time to do it herself, and the tip of her body was all fitted up with the nicest little tool for boring into the ground—the four parts of it pushed down just right, and I think she really liked to use this little boring tool. And of course she really liked to put her precious eggs there in slanting rows in the soft froth that soon hardened about them, keeping them clean and safe all winter.

So her own queer little nest was left in the earth just as her mother's had been,—that good old Earth that takes care of what is planted in her,—the same good old Earth to whom we owe, in many ways, our own life, just as surely as Carol's babies owe theirs to her: even those of us who are far from her, in a city flat way up in the air, instead of down by the country roadside, like a grasshopper in the sun.

CHAPTER IX

ANN GUSTI'S CIRCUS

ANN GUSTI was chewing a buttercup-leaf. If you did such a thing yourself, I dare say it would make your tongue smart a bit. But Ann Gusti belonged to a family of blister beetles, and a peppery salad tasted very good to her. In fact, she liked it better than any other food. For this reason some people name her Buttercup Beetle. Besides that, she is often called Oil Beetle, because she can drop oil out of her joints. And when she was a baby, just hatched from an egg, she was so funny that people said she was a Tri-un-gu-lin, and every time she changed her clothes somebody gave her a new name. So you see that by the time she was grown up she had plenty of them; but I like Ann Gusti best of all.

Before she climbed up the buttercup-stem she put on the very last dress she was ever going to have, and a pretty one it was, too. It fitted her nicely, for, of course, like all beetle dresses, it grew on her body inside the dress she wore before; and when it was ready for her to use, she crept out through a rip in the old one; and there she was, all spick-and-span!

It was a lovely dark-blue color, with some broad

black stripes that were as shiny as satin. And on the back were two wing-covers that did very well for trimming, though they were not of much use, for there were no wings under them.

No, poor Ann Gusti never had a ride with her own wings in her life. But perhaps we need not be sorry for her, because she had one good ride through the air for all that, one day when she was a baby and

Before she climbed up the buttercup stem, she put on her last dress.

her name was Tri-un-gu-lin. As it was one of the most wonderful rides in the world, that was enough to last her a lifetime.

This was the way it happened. When Ann Gusti hatched out of an egg, she was hungry. Of course she was. All babies are hungry, or else they wouldn't eat and grow up; and most insect babies can find something to eat very near at hand.

But Ann Gusti couldn't. That was before she learned to eat buttercup-leaves!

In fact, there was only one sort of food in the whole wide world that would agree with her when she was wee and wore her first baby clothes. Now that food was way, way off in a bee's nest, and she didn't know where

the nest was. Most babies in a fix like that would have starved to death.

But Ann Gusti didn't! Oh, no! She just climbed up into a flower and waited.

By-and-by a bee came buzzing to the flower, and then, quick as a flash, wee Ann Gusti grabbed hold of the hairs on Mother Bee's leg; and that is how she got her ride and that is how she got her breakfast. For she clung tightly to the hairs, and off she rode wherever Mother Bee went, from pretty flower to pretty flower, and at last right into the bee's nest, where she made herself at home and liked the food and stayed.

If you know a smarter baby than Ann Gusti, or a stranger ride to take before the first breakfast, I hope you'll write a story about it.

So with a ride like that to start life with, it is no wonder that Ann Gusti grew up to be a clown in a circus.

Did you think that a circus had to be under a cloth tent, with tigers and lions in cages, and trained horses and dogs there to do tricks?

Well, Jack and Jane liked that kind, too; but they went to a different sort of circus with Uncle David one day as a special treat, and they both said his kind is the best there is.

The top of the tent was the prettiest blue you can ever see, and at one side there were trees with the earliest ripe apples on them, and at another there was a river with a rocky bank and a great flat stone with a bonfire burning on it; and at a third side there was a meadow; but neither Jack nor Jane could tell what was on the fourth side, because Ann Gusti was playing her funny tricks in the meadow; and so that was as far as they got.

As I said to begin with, Ann Gusti was chewing a buttercup-leaf. She was right in plain sight at first, but the minute the toe of Uncle David's boot hit the buttercup-stem she was gone. Now you know she couldn't fly, because she had no wings under her wing-covers; and if a bee had come along just then it would have done no good, for by this time she was grown up and much, much bigger than a bee; so she couldn't have ridden off that way, either.

After a hunt among the leaves she was found on the ground, lying on one side with her head held so close to her body that her yellow neck did not show. Her little feelers were reaching up, but they were still; and her legs looked limp, and there were oily drops coming out at the joints.

"Oh!" said Jane, "she's dropped down dead!"

That shows how Ann Gusti fooled them! That shows how well she could do her trick! No trained dog could have looked deader if he had practised a year!

The children lay down on the ground with their chins in their hands, and waited and waited and waited. Just before their necks ached so that they couldn't wait another minute, Ann Gusti wiggled her toes. Then she moved her feelers the least little bit. Then after a while, as everything was quiet, she got up on her feet and climbed the buttercup-stem and went on chewing a leaf as if there was nothing at all the matter with her. And there wasn't. She was just fooling them. That was Ann Gusti's trick.

"She's a clown!" said Jack.

Ann Gusti wiggled her toes.

And that is how it happened that Ann Gusti had a circus on Labor Day before school began, when the friends of Jack and Jane could come.

The children played the woodshed was a tent. Beside the tent door there was a sign made by cutting big letters out of a newspaper and pasting them on card-board to make the words:—

SIDE SHOW

THREE WONDERS OF THE WORLD

1. ANN GUSTI, THE FAMOUS FAT CLOWN

2. THE THINNEST LIVING SKELETON

3. THE SPRY AMERICAN ACROBAT

Inside there were three cages for the animals. Ann Gusti was in the middle one, chewing buttercup-leaves. And when Jack touched her and said, "Now, you are a dead beetle," she would tumble down to the bottom of the cage and play she was dead—every single time. Good Ann Gusti—she knew her trick and did it, just

95

as her mother and father and all the Gusti family had done as far back as any one can remember! They were all clowns, those Gustis.

The minute they hatched out of their eggs they were ready for their bee-riding trick; and then late in life, when they wore wing-covers that didn't cover any wings, they played they were dead before they were. In fact they had all saved their lives many a time by playing they were dead.

So, being used to this trick, Ann Gusti could do it just as well with everybody watching her as she could out in the field when some bird or little animal came too near.

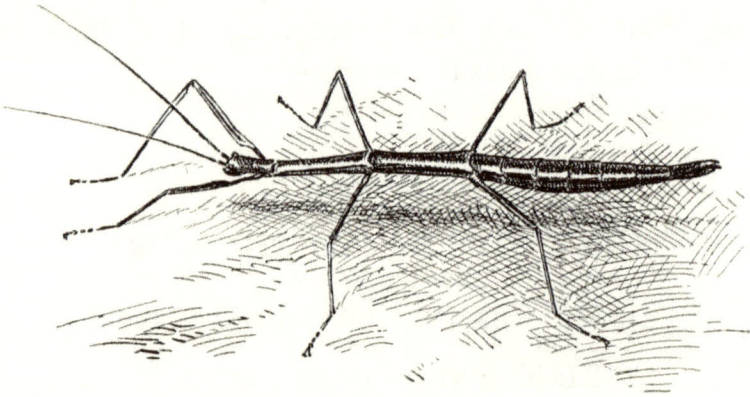

The thinnest living skeleton.

In the cage to the right of Ann Gusti was the "Thinnest Living Skeleton," whose body looked like one little twig and her six thin legs like six others. She was a sort of distant cousin to Carol and Gryl, but you would never think it to look at her. They both had large thick strong jumping hind-legs to hop with, and if the "skeleton" had ever tried to hop, it would have made anybody laugh to see her. But I don't think she ever tried.

As she had no wings or wing-covers whatever, she couldn't fly like Carol and she couldn't fiddle like Gryl.

In fact, there wasn't much she could do but look like a twig. But she did that perfectly! If a person can do just one thing very well indeed, she gets along pretty well in this world. The "skeleton" had always been in a little oak tree before she came to the circus; and if you had tried to see her there, you would have found out that she could hide herself in plain sight on an oak-branch as well as Carol could hide herself in plain sight on the sand. Maybe that's how she came to look so like a twig that people call her a "walking-stick."

In the cage to the left of Ann Gusti was a beetle who had a queer spring on the under side of his body; and whenever he found himself on his back, he had the funniest way of getting on his feet you ever thought of. He would jerk his spring with a "click" sound, and that would throw him way up in the air, and then he would come down right-side up. If he didn't do it the first time trying, he would keep on clicking and jumping until he did.

A beetle who had a queer spring.

So altogether Ann Gusti's side-show pleased the children and did the little animals no harm.

By the next day, though, she became tired of her

cage and tried her best to get out. She climbed up to the top and clung with her six little feet at the crack, and pushed and poked and bumped with her head, trying to find a place where she could squeeze through. If Jack lifted the top, she would stop just where she was as if frightened, and keep still without moving a feeler or toe. When the cover was put down, she would wait a long time, and then begin all over again, creeping round and round and round the top of the cage, clinging at the crack with her feet, and pushing, pushing, pushing, with her hard little head.

That made both Jack and Jane so sorry for her that they gave her back to Uncle David, who took her home to her own wide meadow. And the last that was ever known of Ann Gusti, she had the great big beautiful sky for a circus-tent, and the little clown was chewing a buttercup-leaf whenever she felt hungry.

CHAPTER X

GRYL, THE LITTLE BLACK MINSTREL

A LITTLE bird with a blue back was going in and out of a round hole in an old tree near the river. Now and then he would stop and say "Tru-i-lee, tru-i-lee," very softly to his mate. He sang as if he liked the hole, and perhaps he did; for was this not the place where he and his mate had nested in the spring? And now, before they flew far off to the south, had he not come back again to sit near the old doorway and sing to her?

One tree on the river-bank was red and one was yellow, for it was an October day and their leaves were no longer green. Under them the quiet water seemed red and yellow, too, as if a big looking-glass lay there for the trees to see themselves in.

With a bluebird singing his good-bye song and the gay leaves making bright places in the water, it was a day to be happy in.

And Gryl Cricket was happy, even though he did not listen to the bird or look at the river. He was singing, too, the only song he knew. A funny sort of song it was,

There he sat, the happy little fellow.

with all the words in the verse alike, and every verse just like the one before, and not much change in the tune. But although it was the same music over and over again, it had different sounds for all that. When near by, it was something like "Gr-gryl-l, gr-gryl-l, gr-gryl-l," tinkled oh, so quickly on a tiny bell; and when it was far off, it was more like "Cri-cri-cri-cri."

Whether far or near, it was very good music for an October day. Any way, Gryl liked to make it: you may be sure of that, for he kept at it, off and on, all the warm sunny part of the day. And in the summer, before the nights were so cool, he sang in the dark, too.

With so much singing day after day, does his little black throat ache and his voice grow hoarse?

Not a bit of it; for Gryl's music-box is not like yours and the birds'. It is not in his throat at all! He wears a fiddle on his back and sings, not through his throat,

100

but with his wings.

There he sat, the happy little fellow, before his open door, and fiddled. He lifted two wings and rubbed them together so that the row of tiny hard ridges on the under side of his right wing hit against the hard wrinkles on the upper side of his left wing, and that is the way he made music for himself.

His "Cri-cri-cri" just now seemed to be a song of thankfulness, as hungry people often say "grace" before they eat. Gryl had been too cold to get up for his breakfast, and now it was dinner-time and he was sitting before a feast and fiddling as he ate. "I have meat and I can eat," he seemed to be saying over and over to himself.

If he was glad, it was no wonder; he had found, when he went hunting, a nice fresh leg of grasshopper which a blackbird had dropped near his home. Now Gryl liked a grasshopper-leg as surely as you like a turkey's drumstick for Thanksgiving dinner. So he munched and munched all by himself, and fiddled as he ate.

Sometimes at parties, or in lunch-rooms, we have someone play to us during dinner. But we have to hire our meal-time music. A man can not play a fiddle on his back and eat at the same time. Funny little Gryl could do just that, and it would make you laugh right out loud to see him do it.

The longer Gryl nibbled and fiddled, the more restless Taffy grew. Taffy Cricket, I forgot to say, was Gryl's neighbor, and he lived so near that he could smell

Gryl's marrow-bone; and, like his namesake in the old verse, Taffy was a thief.

Perhaps if Taffy's home had been where the sun warmed it earlier than it did Gryl's, Taffy would have wakened in time to find the bone first. But as it was, he had been too cold and lazy to start out until Gryl was half through his dinner. And the more he smelled that bone, the more he wanted it. So before long he crept out from under the slanting stone that covered his cave, and slipped very quietly in under the old piece of flat tin that made a roof for Gryl's dining-room.

While Gryl was making a merry, noisy tune over his meal, could Taffy come very softly and join the feast?

He tried, and what happened to him was something like what would happen to you if you tried to take away a dog's bone. For wherever a dog has found his bone, he feels very, very sure, in his own mind, that it belongs to him, and no one except his master must go near him while he is eating. If we do, and get hurt, then it is our own fault and we must not blame the dog.

Perhaps Gryl felt that way, for he ran right up to Taffy and scared him off. The funny part of it was that he didn't stop fiddling while he ran! He just lifted his wings higher and fiddled louder, and this time he was not playing gently, "I have meat and I can eat," to himself: he was playing a threat to Taffy which meant, "Taffy Cricket this is my bone. I hunted for it. I found it. I brought it home. You lazy thing, you just go out and hunt for your own dinner. Go away! Go away! Go away!"

Gryl and Taffy

Taffy must have understood him, even though what he said sounded like "cre-ek, cre-ek, cre-ek!" He understood so well that he did not even stop to turn round. He just stepped out backward and left Gryl, as he had found him, fiddling over his dinner.

When Gryl had eaten plenty of food, he washed one of his front feet by putting it into his mouth. Then he pulled one of his long feelers down with his foot, until he could wash that, too. After that he brushed his shiny black sides with his hind-legs; for this was Gryl's wedding-day and of course he must be clean as well as happy.

In the afternoon he went for a walk in the sunshine. He was merry as could be, except when a man happened to come that way and shake the ground with his heavy foot. Then Gryl stopped fiddling and sat so still that even his feelers did not move. He stayed still a long, long time, and then crept off under some fallen leaves, to hide until the steps passed far away. He could never fly even when danger was near. His front wings were a fiddle and his hind ones weak, little folded things that were too feeble to carry him an inch. But he knew how to slip away and hide, as you would find if you tried to catch him for a pet.

Toward night he played a soft tune to Lucy Cricket, who lived under a bit of bark near his own little dug-out.

Now Lucy was black as a piece of coal, and her head was so bald and shiny that not a hair could be seen on it anywhere, and she was dumb.

But she was not deaf, and she could hear Gryl's song and liked it. And what do you suppose she did? Do you think she painted her little black cheeks and put on a wig? Oh, no; she was an honest cricket and went out to her mate just as she was. As he was black as a piece of coal, too, and just as bald as she was, they really looked very much alike, except that her wings had no fiddles, and he had no long slender tail, but only two tail-feathers.

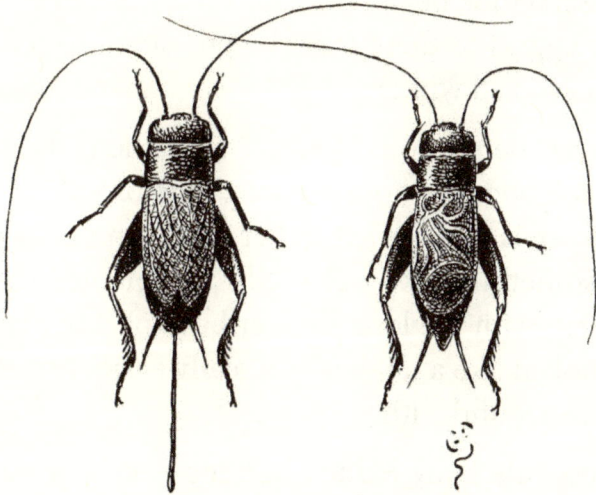

Lucy and Gryl Cricket

Well, Gryl went right on fiddling, and this time it was their wedding march. For a wedding supper they had a wild-lettuce salad, with some apple-sauce for dessert; for there was a wild-apple tree on the bank, and the apples that had dropped down were nice and soft.

Then Lucy went back to her cave under the bark and Gryl found his way to his own little dug-out.

After all, he did not need any one to help him about his meals. He rather liked going out to hunt for them himself. And he needed no one to show him how to finish his dug-out. He knew just how to pick up the hard little bit of dirt or stone in his mouth and carry it off out of the way, and just how to scratch out the soft places with his head and feet.

It was well that he felt that way about it, for Lucy was far too busy with her own task to help Gryl or any one else. It took her all her time for a while to take care of her eggs. For these must be put down so that they would keep all winter.

What better could she do with them than trust them to good old Mother Earth, who broods over the tiniest seeds that are left in her care? And Lucy's eggs were something like wee seeds. She planted them in the earth with the long slender back part of her body, that looked like a tail but was really a tool to put eggs into the ground with.

So while Lucy tended her eggs like a good little mother, Gryl finished his dug-out, making it deeper and deeper, until the days grew very cold and he fell asleep in his bedroom in the same earth that sheltered Lucy's eggs.

One day, a long time after that, the trees, which had dropped their red and yellow leaves on the river-bank, unfolded some very fresh green ones. A bird with a blue back, who had flown far, far to the south, and north again, was hopping in and out of the hole in the old tree near by and whispering "Tru-i-lee, tru-i-lee" sweetly to his mate.

It was spring, and time for Gryl to waken from his long nap and begin fiddling again. For there are always some crickets to welcome the spring—their songs do not belong just to the summer and fall.

As Gryl sat and fiddled before his open door, his little sons and daughters hatched in their egg-shells and climbed up out of the ground.

They were wee midgets who looked much like old Daddy Gryl, with their bald black heads and hopping hind-legs. For a cricket is a cricket all the days of his life except while he is an egg. He isn't one thing first and then another afterward, like a caterpillar turning into a butterfly.

All a small cricket has to change to is a larger cricket. So there was not a great deal of difference between Gryl and one of his little sons except size and wings. For a baby cricket is like all other baby insects, who must eat and grow up before they can have any wings.

While he is growing, he must throw off his little black skin when it gets too tight, and from time to time his wing-pads will get bigger. Then, when he changes his skin the last time, there will be wings on his back instead of pads—not wings to fly with, but to fiddle with.

So, long before the bluebird will come to say good-bye to his nest next October, Daddy Gryl's sons will be fiddling near their open doors, merrily, oh merrily, as crickets should.

CHAPTER XI

LUNA'S THANKSGIVING

THE hazelnut bushes had dropped their leaves. They were dry brown leaves now, that rustled when the boys and girls waded through them; and when the wind lifted them up and made them dance, they flew here and there as if they were merry.

But there was one leaf that did not dance with the others. It stayed still, for it was wrapped tightly about Luna's little silk-room. Luna had papered the outside of her room with the leaf before she spun the wall too thick to reach through. Now you can tell from that that Luna was a caterpillar; because what else could it be that would spin a room of silk?

Yes, Luna had been a caterpillar once upon a time in her spinning days—a big one, too, and a pretty one, a very, very pretty one. But after she had finished making her little home that had just one room in it, she rested a while and then she stopped being a caterpillar. It happened this way. Her last caterpillar clothes ripped down a back seam just behind her head, and her caterpillar skull cracked open like a nut. And the pale little body that lay inside was not a caterpillar any more.

No, Luna was a pupa now, and grew darker and darker until she was brown all over. There was nothing for her to do but to sleep, for her one room was a bedroom, and she had locked herself in until spring.

Luna had been a caterpillar once upon a time,
and a pretty one.

There was no pantry in her little house, and she could not eat. Not one crumb of food and not one drop of drink was she to have all winter. But she was so plump that we need not feel sorry for her, for she had spent all her life in a pantry until she made her bedroom, and had eaten enough to last her a long, long time. Her pantry had been an oak tree, and the shelves were the oak-leaves, and she ate up some of the shelves!

Before she was a caterpillar she was a white egg; and her mother, who was very beautiful indeed, had put this white egg with some others on top of one of the oak-leaf shelves. This made it handy for Luna when she nibbled a hole in the egg-shell and poked her little head out. What more could she want than to be hatched in a pantry with so much food in it that she could eat whenever she felt hungry? And an oak pantry, too! She wouldn't have minded if she had hatched in a birch or walnut pantry, but there was nothing she liked better than oak. Indeed, she liked an oak-leaf as well as a blue jay or a squirrel likes an acorn—maybe even better.

So of course she ate and ate, and I think she would have eaten for sixty days without stopping, except for one thing. That one thing was her skin. It was a funny sort of skin to have. It could stretch and grow for about a week, and then it would stop. Whenever Luna's skin stopped stretching she had to stop eating. As soon as this happened, she would spin a thin silk mat all spread out on the leaf, and tangle the little hooks on her ten fat clinging feet in it, and wait. While she waited she would lift her head and put her six thin front-legs together, so that she looked as if she were asking for something.

What she needed was a new skin that would stretch farther, and a new head so that she could eat bigger slices of good oak-leaves.

And sure enough she was going to have them both! For there behind her head that was too little for her, there was a place where her neck looked swollen. That was because a new head was growing inside her old tight skin; and as it grew, it pushed the little old skull off until it looked something like the nose-bags men put on their horses when they feed them away from home, where there is no food-box.

And at last her bigger new head inside her skin pushed the little old skull so far that rip, rip went the skin right round her collar, and off dropped the little old skull and out popped her new head! Then she crept out of the old tight skin through the collar-hole; and there she was as good as new, with a new suit of skin that would stretch for about a week. So she could eat another good long meal.

That was the way she ate and grew, and that was the way she changed her skin-dress. And every dress she had was a little different from the one she had before. They were all pretty dresses, and all green ones that did not show much when she was clinging to her green pantry shelves. The tips of her legs were reddish brown, and so was her mouth. She had some tiny red dots and some yellow ones on her dress, and some blue ones. There was a yellow line along each side and some in other places. These colors made her all the prettier, but they did not show very far away, and she really looked nearly as green as the leaves she ate.

When she had on her last suit of skin, she grew to be three inches long; and when she was about sixty days old, she left the oak pantry for the first time in her life. And she was never going back. Plenty of good fresh leaves lay all about her on every side; but greedy as she had been all her growing days, she seemed to know when she had had enough and did not stop to take another bite. She walked along the branch until she came to the trunk of the tree, and then down she crept head first—way to the ground. Then she wandered off for her very first walk on the ground.

111

The moonbeams could find nothing lovelier than Luna.

It was her very last one, too; for by the time she had reached a hazelnut bush she felt like spinning. It was more than a thin mat to rest on, while she changed her dress, that she felt like making. There was a leaf near by and she felt like spinning this about her with silk and making her cocoon inside it. Cocoon is the name of her bedroom.

The silk she used dripped out of a tube near her under-lip. It was wet and sticky at first, but as soon as the air touched it, it hardened into a fine thread. She spun these threads in little loops by swinging her head from side to side, and it took more loops than you can count to make enough to cover her all up, though the more she spun the shorter she grew. She seemed to shrink as she worked; and by the time the cocoon was done, it did not have to be more than an inch and a half to hold her.

That is how she came to be all snugly tucked up in a silk cocoon with a leaf wrapped about it. Then she changed to a little pupa inside, as brown as the hazelnuts the children were hunting.

For it was Thanksgiving time, and Jack and Jane were nutting in Uncle David's woods. But Luna did not hear them as they laughed and shouted and waded through the dry leaves, any more than she heard the big black birds calling "Caw! caw!" or the other big bird with a jacket almost as blue as the sky, scream at the top of his lungs that his name was "Jay! Ja-ay!" The woods might ring with noises, but Luna slept on. Boys and girls might have turkey baked brown and

She would fly in the moonlight.

cranberries cooked to a beautiful red jelly and candy with hazelnuts in it for their Thanksgiving dinner. What did Luna care about that? She had eaten her fill long ago. The only Thanksgiving she needed was to sleep safely in her cocoon. That is how she spent the day. Alone and asleep! Sometimes she wiggled and turned in her bed, but she did not waken. She would wait until Spring called her, and then her long, long night would be over.

Then she would break her brown pupa case and wet her cocoon with something that would soften the hard silk so that she could break her way through, and out she would come—out of her bedroom into the open world of sunshine and moonlight!

At first her wings would be tiny limp flaps, and they would grow bigger and bigger and bigger until it would take a ruler five inches long to reach across them when they were spread. And they would grow so fast you could see them do it!

Their color would be the loveliest pale green there is in the world. Near the middle of each one there would be a tiny clear place, like a wee window with a pretty frame of white, black, and red. Across the front edge of the front wings would be a border of purple, and the hind wings would each end in a long part like a tail.

Luna's body lying between the wings would be covered by beautiful white fluffy scales, the whitest white that ever was seen—whiter even than the feathers on a white dove! Upon her head would wave two pale brown plumes. There she would be next summer—a moth so lovely that you would not want to touch her, but just look and look and look.

What would she do, this wonderful green and white and purple moth who had been a plump, brown sleeping pupa before that, and a pretty, growing caterpillar, green as an oak-leaf, before that, and a white egg first of all?

She would fly in the woodland, but not by day. She was a moon moth and would wait for night to come.

By night she would fly, and where, do you think? To the flowers with deep cups, and uncoil her long tongue to sip up the sweet drops at the bottom? Oh, no. That is what many moths would do, but Luna had no tongue and could not drink. That is the way Lunas are made. They eat, when they are caterpillars, enough to last them while they sleep the sleep of change. All moths are like that. But Luna's caterpillar food lasts her all her life, though many other moths sip from flowers at night as butterflies do by day.

No, Luna would not visit the blossoms that hold up their sweet-smelling cups. She would fly—have you guessed where?

Yes, she would fly in the moonlight.

She would be beautiful enough to be a fairy, with her snowy robe and her pale green wings. You could call her a fairy princess if you liked, and say that her name is Princess Luna. And the prince would come to fly near her in the moonlight. Be sure of that—Prince Luna would be there, too. He would be dressed like the princess, with a white robe and fair green wings, and the plumes on his head would be even larger than hers. The moonbeams seeking through all the woods could find nothing lovelier than the Prince and Princess Luna.

There would be music for the night-time. In the fields near by, a black cricket would be fiddling joyfully. Way, way off, a night bird would call. The brook would make a sweet tune as it ran over the stones in its path. And overhead the oak-leaves would be whispering.

Would they call the princess, do you think? Or was there a fragrance in the whispering leaves that drew her to them? In some strange way the oak would tell her to come, and she would fly back to the tree she left so many months before. There upon the leaves she would put her eggs, her most precious gift to the world; and they would gleam in the moonlight like fairy pearls.

Later there must be cocoons wrapped in fallen leaves.

She had been like one of them herself a year before. And if, in the year to follow, there are to be Prince and Princess Lunas floating among the moonbeams, there must be pearly eggs upon the oak-leaves, just as later there must be cocoons wrapped in fallen leaves, each with a pupa in it brown as a nut at Thanksgiving time.

CHAPTER XII

KETI ABBOT

The Littlest Christmas Guest

Keti Abbot lived all alone in a tiny log cabin in a holly tree. Sometimes a wonderful cardinal bird sat on the branches near him and sang, his gay feathers looking very pretty against the glossy green leaves; for you know how becoming red is to a holly twig.

Now Keti's father and mother had never kept house in the log cabin where he lived, and he had never seen either of them. Mrs. Abbot had left his egg, with a lot of others, in her own log cabin on a holly branch; and that was about all she had ever been able to do for her son. But you must not be sorry for the little orphan, for from the moment he hatched Keti was able to take care of himself. He had, in fact, never known an unhappy hour. He had everything he needed—a snug little home and plenty of food; and he never would have been lonesome even if the cardinal bird had not come there at all. But as this singer was not making sweet music to give him joy, the feelings of the bird were not hurt when Keti did not listen to him.

Keti lived all alone in a tiny log cabin.

Keti was so busy getting his meals and building his log cabin that little else mattered to him, just so he was let alone as his father and mother had left him. It seems strange to think of that little chap finding food for himself from the time he was a baby less than a day old and ready for his first bite. Yet very soon after he had poked his head out of the egg-shell, he had crept off and fed himself on a nice crisp holly-leaf salad. It agreed with him better than malted milk would have done, which you may be very sure was the reason Mrs. Abbot had placed her precious eggs where she did. If her son was to be left to find his own food, she would at least see to it that he was put where he would not starve for lack of the proper kind.

That was all very well so far as his meals went; but where was the carpenter to be found who would make him a snug cabin? For, after he crept out of the egg-shell, he had no covering for his tender little body, and no son of the House of Abbot would be caught without just the right sort of shelter over his head. No, indeed. His family for many, many years back had all had tidy places of their own, and it was not to be thought for a moment that he would get along without one as good as any of them had had. He might be fatherless and motherless, and with no nurse to prepare his dinner for him; but homeless he would not be. Never! And he didn't sit round waiting for that carpenter, either. He went to work as busy as a little bee and made his own log cabin. That is what Keti did. Think of it,—with no one to show him how,—and he a baby just new in the world! He started it with the tiniest pieces, for he was wee himself and did not need a big dwelling; and if you had seen him turning heels over head with it in the beginning, you might have thought that he was only playing a game with a cunning little collar. But he kept at it until it covered him all up, and as fast as he grew, he kept chopping more tiny holly logs and making it bigger, to fit him.

He cut the wee twig-logs as neatly as a man could cut huge ones with an axe, although he had no choppers to use but his own strong jaws. He placed them criss-cross at the ends, and fastened them together firmly, not with wooden pegs or nails, but with silk.

Now, no man who is not very rich has his walls covered with silk, for it costs a great deal to buy it. But it was none too good for Keti Abbot, who would have as fine a cabin as his father and his grandfather and his great-grandfather had had, even if he did have to make every bit himself. You will wonder where he got his silk. It grew in a sort of pocket in his body back of his head, and all he had to do when he was ready to spin was to pull it out from an opening in his mouth and swing it back and forth until he wove a silken lining for his little log cabin of a nest. And no one taught him how to spin or how to weave. He just did it all right the first time he tried.

After he had taken all that pains with his home, you will not be surprised to learn that he liked it so well that he stayed in it night and day, never leaving it for a minute all the fall. He no more left that little log case of his than a snail would leave her shell, and in some ways he got along in much the same way that a snail does. When he went walking about on the highroads of the holly branches, he stuck his head and creeping feet out of the open doorway and stepped off—cabin and all. While he was tiny, he walked on top of the branch, with his house straight up in the air; but after he grew and his house was too heavy to hold that way, he traveled on the under-side of the branch and let his home hang down like a bag.

He travelled on the under side of the branch and let his home hang down like a bag.

In this way he would hunt here and there about the tree for the best holly salads; and having his dwelling handy by, he could camp out wherever he happened to be.

Now all these things that Keti did without any practice—like catching his own salad at just the right stage, and cutting holly-twigs just the right length, and fitting them together at the corners in just the right way, and binding them into a snug little home with a silken lining which he spun and wove just right—are very wonderful things indeed. And perhaps it is not quite true to say that he was not taught, because, after all, he had a better teacher than can be found in all the colleges of the world, or even in all the kindergartens. Of course that famous teacher is Dame Nature herself; and the little chap got along so well with all the hard lessons of his life by simply obeying his instincts.

It isn't much use to pucker up your brow and try to understand how Dame Nature led Keti from task to task, and how he could do all these things perfectly the first time trying. You might study about it for more than one hundred years, and even then not understand very well. It is enough for us to know that Keti ate and cut and builded and spun and wove; so much any of us can find out for ourselves by some day watching one of his kind; for Keti grew up in time, and had children and grandchildren and great-grandchildren; and although he never saw any of them himself, that is no reason why we cannot see them.

It was during the fall, when Keti was only a few weeks old, that the cardinal bird sat in the holly tree now and then, adding his bright feathers to the bright berries on the twig and making altogether a lovely picture, though Keti never noticed the gay visitor when he poked his head out of his cabin door.

Neither did he see those little cousins of his on the trees near by, who were making other kinds of cases

Keti's cousins.

to live in. They were not such pretty ones as Keti's, and
the sticks went up and down on the outside instead of
crosswise, and perhaps they looked more like bags than
log cabins. Still they did as well for shelter, and were
as carefully lined with silk. One was as large as Keti's
home, but the others were much smaller. Each made
his house in his own way, and never looked to see what
his cousin was doing.

So Keti worked at building and spinning day by day;

and he walked here and there along the holly highroad, clinging to the under side of the branch, whenever he felt hungry enough to hunt up a good fresh dinner.

Well, after a while the weather grew colder—as cold, indeed, as it ever gets in the land where Keti lived; for winter came on and the little fellow, still less than four months old, was growing drowsy. So he fastened his cabin to a twig with silk, and swung there like a bird in a nest while he took rather a long nap. He was safe as a baby oriole in his swinging house, which rocked in the wind like the cradle old Mother Goose once sang about.

And after he had slept there a number of weeks, three children ran along one day, looking for holly branches to make their house bright at Christmastime. Little Eleanor spied Keti's cabin swinging like a cradle and said, "Oh my! oh my! oh me! oh my! Here's a tiny wee bag of sticks! I want it for Dolly Jane's very own little Christmas-tree. And there is a holly-berry stuck right in the side of it!"

So David took out his knife and cut off Keti's cabin, twig and all; and Eleanor tucked it among the branches of a small evergreen tree which she was making ready for Dolly Jane's Christmas.

There Keti stayed while Eleanor and David and Phoebe helped make laurel wreaths, and while Father put up the big red balls, and while Mother hurried about making plum pudding and wonderful cakes and candies.

On December twenty-fourth the three children

crept away to bed very early, so as to be sure not to be too sleepy to waken if they should hear anything that sounded like reindeer stamping on the roof or any jingle that might be sleigh-bells; for Mother always read to them,—

> 'Twas the night before Christmas,
> When all through the house
> Not a creature was stirring—
> Not even a mouse,—

and the rest of those jolly verses, every Christmas Eve; and every time they could not help thinking how amusing it would be to see for themselves what really happened in their own home on that night so full of secrets.

But it was not Eleanor or David or Phoebe who wakened that Christmas Eve. It was little Keti, who crept off Dolly Jane's tree right in the midst of all the fun. The house was so warm that he got over being drowsy, and suddenly the electric lights were turned on, which made the room bright as day.

And there was Somebody putting glitter all over the big Christmas tree until it sparkled like stars and icicles and shiny snow. And there were bright toy birds perched on the twigs, and ropes of gayest red and pretty gold and silver hanging all about the spreading green branches. And all around the base of the tree was a long line of toy animals like every kind you can see at the circus. A little reindeer led them, and after him came all the others, like a grand parade.

And Somebody was cramming the stockings by

the fireplace so full of little packages that they were all bunched out. And there were toys and books and bundles tied with red ribbon in piles before the grate. And Somebody kept laughing softly and whispering, "Eleanor will love to swing Dolly Jane in this little hammock"; and "David will make wonderful things with this set of carpenter tools"; and "Phoebe will paint pictures in this book by the hour."

Think of it! All those things happening while the three children slept soundly, and little Keti Abbot awake all that delightful Christmas Eve! He even felt so lively that he crept out to the nearest holly-branch and nibbled a lunch at midnight.

And fly forth to seek out a wingless mate.

While he was doing this, Somebody saw him creeping about and chuckled, and then shook a finger at him and called him a long name that sounded like talking in Latin. "Oiketicus abbotii," Somebody whispered, "don't tell what you have seen to-night. It's a secret, you know." And sure enough, Keti, the little Christmas guest of Dolly Jane, never told a soul about what went on that gay night, although he crept from place to place and feasted during the twelve days before the holly, with him on it, was taken out-doors again. Then he went to sleep until warm weather came, and wakened him to eat and grow and change into a little winged creature like his father, and fly forth to seek out a wingless mate in a log cabin like the one his mother had once lived in.

A WORD TO THE TEACHER

IF you are an out-door sort of person, you will find ways of your own of sharing and adding to the natural interest of the child in the habits of living creatures, whether they be two-, four-, or six-footed; and your own ways will be better for you than those that anyone else can suggest.

If, however, you think that you have no enthusiasm for the various phases of the subject called Nature Study, you may find that the easiest as well as the frankest way to deal with the situation is simply not to try to "teach" it at all. Let the child learn for himself (there is perhaps no better way), taking care only to be as sympathetic and responsive as you honestly can. If Tom brings in a caterpillar, let him keep it in a glass jar on the table or window-sill, if he is willing to keep it supplied with leaves and to wash and wipe the jar daily. The top can be fastened down securely, which will keep the leaves moist and fresh; and the supply of air will be all, and more than, the insect needs. A clean glass jar, with a tight top and with a piece of soft paper in the bottom, is a good cage. The pet can be watched; there is no danger of its being lost in the room, and it is not an unsightly object to have about. If Dick catches a pair of crickets, a similar jar, with earth in the bottom and a slice of apple or such other food as Dick finds his pet will eat, will make both boy and insects happy, and the little black fiddler can be watched at his music, and his mate as she lays her eggs in the dirt. If Harriet comes in with a chrysalis, a third jar will keep it safe until the "grand opening" day. Perhaps three jars will be enough of an insectary for the schoolroom, though if some other child has a different sort of Hexapod at home, it might be allowed to come for a visit some day.

The six-footed creatures are, in many ways, better subjects for the beginning lessons in Nature Study than most other animals, or plants. And children like them, unless they are taught by some foolish grown-up that it is nice to shudder at anything that creeps. The longer the child can hold fast to his early liking for these denizens of out-of-doors (and some of us never lose it), the deeper his joyful interest in woodland, field, and roadside rambles will be; and it is an unfriendly and an unkind act to mar this natural pleasure.

As for the references that follow, it may be said that the length of the list need not be appalling. It is not likely that any teacher will have both time and inclination to read all of them. It is not necessary, so far as the stories in this book are concerned, to read any of them. But some teachers will want to read some of them, and some librarians will be glad to see that they are available. So they are offered, not as a burden for those who do not wish, or have not time to use them, but as a reference aid for those who are interested to read what others have written about the insects of the stories or related subjects.

NOTES

I. VAN, THE SLEEPY BUTTERFLY

Euvanessa antiopa: the Mourning Cloak. This butterfly belongs to the family called the Nymphs. The first six references concern directly the butterfly of the story; the others give topics of interest in connection with it.

JULIA P. BALLARD. *Among the Moths and Butterflies.* (G. P. Putnam's Sons.) Chapter IV: "The Early Butterfly."

JOHN HENRY COMSTOCK and ANNA BOTSFORD COMSTOCK. *How to Know the Butterflies.* (D. Appleton & Co.) Pages 148-151.

MARY C. DICKERSON. *Moths and Butterflies.* (Ginn & Co.) "The Mourning Cloak": pages 69-76.

WILLIAM HAMILTON GIBSON. *Sharp Eyes.* (Harper & Brothers.) "A Butterfly Serenade": pages 30-33; and "The Thaw Butterflies": pages 270-273.

SAMUEL HUBBARD SCUDDER. *Everyday Butterflies.* (Houghton Mifflin Co.) Pages 1-6.

CLARENCE MOORES WEED. *Stories of Insect Life*: First Series. (Ginn & Co.) Pages 22-24.

WILLIAM HAMILTON GIBSON. *Blossom Hosts and Insect Guests.* (Newson & Co.) "How the Flowers Woo the Insects": pages 19-36.

JOSEPH LANE HANCOCK. *Nature Sketches in Temperate America.* (A. C. McClurg & Co.) Chapter III: "Protective Resemblance."

DAVID STARR JORDAN AND VERNON L. KELLOGG. *Animal Life.* (D. Appleton & Co.) Chapter XII: "Protective Resemblances."

JOHN H. LOVELL. *The Flower and the Bee.* (Charles Scribner's Sons.) "Butterfly Flowers": pages 125-138.

CLARENCE MOORES WEED. *Ten New England Blossoms and their Insect Visitors.* (Houghton Mifflin Co.) "The Mayflower": pages 18-31.

II. OLD BUMBLE

ANNA BOTSFORD COMSTOCK. *Handbook of Nature Study.* (Comstock Pub. Co.) "The Bumblebees": pages 442-444.

WILLIAM HAMILTON GIBSON. *Sharp Eyes.* (Harper & Brothers.) "Queer Fruits from the Bee's Basket": pages 112-116.

WILLIAM HAMILTON GIBSON. *Blossom Hosts and Insect Guests.* (Newson & Co.) "How the Flowers Woo the Insects": pages 19-36; "The Barberry's Welcome to Master Bombus": pages 37-42; and "The Wood-Betony, a Protégé of the Bumblebee": pages 85-90.

Joseph Lane Hancock. *Nature Sketches in Temperate America.* (A. C. McClurg & Co.) "The Bumblebees' Night Camp": pages 304-306.

Vernon L. Kellogg. *American Insects.* (Henry Holt & Co.) Chapter XVI: "Insects and Flowers."

John H. Lovell. *The Flower and the Bee.* (Charles Scribner's Sons.) Chapter V: "Bumblebee Flowers"; and Chapter VI: "The Gathering of the Nectar."

Margaret Warner Morley. *The Bee People.* (A. C. McClurg & Co.) Chapter XX: "Bombus, the Bumblebee."

James G. Needham. *Outdoor Studies.* (American Book Co.) "Butter and Eggs and Bumblebees": pages 7-12.

Edith M. Patch. *Dame Bug and Her Babies.* (Pine Cone Pub. Co.) Chapter XIV: "Widow Velvet's May Day."

F. W. L. Sladen. *The Humble-bee.* (Macmillan & Co., London.)

Clarence Moores Weed. *Ten New England Blossoms and their Insect Visitors.* (Houghton Mifflin Co.) "The Mayflower": pages 18-31.

III. CECID

Anna Botsford Comstock. *Handbook of Nature Study.* (Comstock Pub. Co.) "The Gall-dwellers": pages 360-364.

KATHERINE CREIGHTON. *Nature Songs and Stories.* (Comstock Pub. Co.) "The Chickadee": pages 3-5.

WILLIAM HAMILTON GIBSON. *Sharp Eyes.* (Harper & Brothers.) "That Willow Cone": pages 207-209.

VERNON L. KELLOGG. *American Insects.* (Henry Holt & Co.) "Houses of Oak": pages 283-298.

JAMES G. NEEDHAM. *Outdoor Studies.* (American Book Co.) "Houses that Grow": pages 18-29.

EDITH M. PATCH. *Dame Bug and Her Babies.* (Pine Cone Pub. Co.) Chapter I: "The Magic Cone of Cecid."

Because the writer of this story lived where the Cecid cones were common on *Salix cordata*, and the artist lived where they were found on *Salix discolor*, two types are presented to the reader, who may find one or both. Those of the pictures are not so fuzzy as those of the story, and the scales are more inclined to be pointed.

IV. POLY, THE EASTER BUTTERFLY

Papilio polexenes: the Black Swallowtail.

ANNA BOTSFORD COMSTOCK. *Handbook of Nature Study.* (Comstock Pub. Co.) "The Black Swallow-tail Butterfly": pages 315-319.

JOHN HENRY COMSTOCK and ANNA BOTSFORD COMSTOCK. *How to Know the Butterflies.* (D. Appleton & Co.) "The Black Swallowtail": pages 62-65.

MARY C. DICKERSON. *Moths and Butterflies.* (Ginn & Co.) "The Black Swallowtail": pages 39-53.

JUSTUS WATSON FOLSOM. *Entomology.* (P. Blakiston's Son & Co.) Chapter VI: "Adaptive Coloration."

WILLIAM HAMILTON GIBSON. *Blossom Hosts and Insect Guests.* (Newson & Co.) "How the Flowers Woo the Insects": pages 19-36; and "Nature's Inexhaustible Treasures": pages 167-179.

WILLIAM HAMILTON GIBSON. *Sharp Eyes.* (Harper & Brothers.) "Butterfly Botany Teachers": pages 80-86.

JOSEPH LANE HANCOCK. *Nature Sketches in Temperate America.* (A. C. McClurg & Co.) "Warning Colors": pages 137-164.

ERNEST INGERSOLL. *The Wit of the Wild.* (Dodd, Mead & Co.) "Animals that Advertise": pages 102-108.

VERNON L. KELLOGG. *American Insects.* (Henry Holt & Co.) Chapter XVI: "Insects and Flowers"; and Chapter XVII: "Color and Pattern and Their Uses."

JOHN H. LOVELL. *The Flower and the Bee.* (Charles Scribner's Sons.) "Butterfly-Flowers": pages 125-138.

JAMES G. NEEDHAM. *General Biology.* (Comstock Pub. Co.) "Warning Coloration": pages 429-430.

EDITH M. PATCH. *Dame Bug and Her Babies.* (Pine Cone Pub. Co.) Chapter III: "Prince and Princess Swallowtail."

Samuel Hubbard Scudder. *Everyday Butterflies.* (Houghton Mifflin Co.). "The Black Swallowtail": pages 130-137.

H. W. Shepheard-Walwyn. *Nature's Riddles.* (Cassell & Co.) "The Chrysalis State": pages 193-204.

V. JUMPING JACK

W. D. Funkhouser. *Biology of the Membracidæ of the Cayuga Lake Basin*; Memoir 11, Cornell Univ. Agr. Exp. Sta. "Enchenopa binotata."

William Hamilton Gibson. *Eye Spy.* (Harper & Brothers.) "A Queer Little Family on the Bitter-Sweet." First printed in Harper's Magazine, volume 87, pages 432-436.

Ignaz Matausch. "Observations on the Life History of *Enchenopa binotata*," in Journal New York Entomological Society, Volume 20, pages 58-67.

VI. NATA THE NYMPH

Plathemis lydia is Nata's learned name; and Nat is sometimes called the "white-tail."

Anna Botsford Comstock. *Handbook of Nature Study.* (Comstock Pub. Co.) "The Dragon-flies and Damsel-flies": pages 380-386.

Joseph Lane Hancock. *Nature Sketches in*

Temperate America. (A. C. McClurg & Co.) "The Pond": pages 278-283.

VERNON L. KELLOGG. *Insect Stories*. (Henry Holt & Co.) "The Dragon of Lagunita": pages 123-146.

VERNON L. KELLOGG. *American Insects*. (Henry Holt & Co.) Chapter VI: "Dragon-flies and Damsel-flies."

JAMES G. NEEDHAM. *Outdoor Studies*. (American Book Co.) "Dragon Flies": pages 54-72.

EDITH M. PATCH. *Dame Bug and Her Babies*. (Pine Cone Pub. Co.) Chapter X: "The Masker."

VII. LAMPY

ANNA BOTSFORD COMSTOCK. *Handbook of Nature Study*. (Comstock Pub. Co.) "The Firefly": pages 416-418.

WILLIAM HAMILTON GIBSON. *Blossom Hosts and Insect Guests*. (Newson & Co.) "The Evening Primrose": pages 49-60.

WILLIAM HAMILTON GIBSON. *Sharp Eyes*. (Harper & Brothers.) "What the Midnight can Show Us": pages 121-127.

MARY E. MURTFELDT AND CLARENCE MOORES WEED. *Stories of Insect Life*, Second Series. (Ginn & Co.) "The Firefly": pages 14-17.

VIII. CAROL

Carol—otherwise *Dissosteira carolina*—and some of her relatives are concerned with the following accounts.

ANNA BOTSFORD COMSTOCK. *Handbook of Nature Study*. (Comstock Pub. Co.) "The Grasshopper": pages 365-370.

ANNA BOTSFORD COMSTOCK. *Ways of the Six-Footed*. (Ginn & Co.) Pages 15-17.

J. HENRI FABRE. *The Life of the Grasshopper*. (Dodd, Mead & Co.) Chapters XVII, XVIII, and XIX: "The Locusts."

JUSTUS WATSON FOLSOM. *Entomology*. (P. Blakiston's Son & Co.) Chapter VI: "Adaptive Coloration."

JOSEPH LANE HANCOCK. *Nature Sketches in Temperate America*. (A. C. McClurg & Co.) "Protective Resemblance": pages 67-114; and "The Carolina Locust": pages 340-347.

MARGARET WARNER MORLEY. *Grasshopper Land*. (A. C. McClurg & Co.)

JAMES G. NEEDHAM. *General Biology*. (Comstock Pub. Co.) "Resemblance and Flash Colors": pages 423-429.

EDITH M. PATCH. *Dame Bug and Her Babies*. (Pine Cone Pub. Co.) Chapter VII: "Grasshopper Brown."

IX. ANN GUSTI'S CIRCUS

Meloe angusticollis, the buttercup oil-beetle; *Diapheromera femorata*, the walking-stick; and *Alaus oculatus*, the eyed elater.

JOHN HENRY COMSTOCK and ANNA BOTSFORD COMSTOCK. *Manual for the Study of Insects.* (Comstock Pub. Co.) Pages 108, 547, and 588.

JUSTUS WATSON FOLSOM. *Entomology.* (P. Blakiston's Son & Co.) "Protective Resemblance": page 217.

WILLIAM HAMILTON GIBSON. *Eye Spy.* (Harper & Brothers.) "The Story of the Floundering Beetle": pages 1-10.

JOSEPH LANE HANCOCK. *Nature Sketches in Temperate America.* (A. C. McClurg & Co.) "The Habits of the Walking-Stick": pages 76-82.

DAVID STARR JORDAN AND VERNON L. KELLOGG. *Animal Life.* (D. Appleton & Co.) "Special Protective Resemblance": pages 207-212.

VERNON L. KELLOGG. *American Insects.* (Henry Holt & Co.) Pages 131, 268, 289-293.

JAMES G. NEEDHAM. *Outdoor Studies.* (American Book Co.) "Bogus Eyes": pages 74-75.

EDITH M. PATCH. *Dame Bug and Her Babies.* (Pine Cone Pub. Co.) Chapter XII: "The Strange Ride of Triungulin."

CLARENCE MOORES WEED. *Life Histories of American Insects*. (The Macmillan Co.) "The Click-Beetles": pages 29-41.

X. GRYL, THE LITTLE BLACK MINSTREL.

The following references about *Gryllus*, the Cricket, will be interesting.

ANNA BOTSFORD COMSTOCK. *Handbook of Nature Study*. (Comstock Pub. Co.) "The Black Cricket": pages 372-376.

ANNA BOTSFORD COMSTOCK. *Ways of the Six-Footed*. (Ginn & Co.) Chapter I: "Pipers and Minnesingers."

KATHERINE CREIGHTON. *Nature Songs and Stories* (Comstock Pub. Co.) "The Cricket's Song": pages 7-9.

J. HENRI FABRE. *The Life of the Grasshopper*. (Dodd, Mead & Co.) Chapters XV and XVI: "The Cricket."

MARGARET WARNER MORLEY. *Grasshopper Land*. (A. C. McClurg & Co.) Chapter XIX.

XI. LUNA

JULIA P. BALLARD. *Among the Moths and Butterflies*. (G. P. Putnam's Sons.) Chapter XXIII: "A Barrel Full of Lunas."

IDA M. ELIOT and CAROLINE GRAY SOULE. *Caterpillars and Their Moths*. (The Century Co.) Pages 258-261.

Gene Stratton-Porter. *Moths of the Limberlost.* (Doubleday, Page & Co.) "Moths of the Moon": pages 173-188.

H. W. Shepheard-Walwyn. *Nature's Riddles.* (Cassell & Co.) "Silk from the Caterpillar's Point of View": pages 205-222.

XII. KETI ABBOT, THE LITTLEST CHRISTMAS GUEST

Keti's full name is *Oiketicus abbotii* Grote, and he belongs to the family Psychidæ. Keti and his relatives, on account of their curious habits, have such nicknames as "bag-worms," "basket-carriers," and "firewood billies"; and an interesting belief concerning these little creatures is common in Ceylon and in our own Southern States. Two of Keti's cousins, *Thyridopteryx ephemerœformis*, and *Psyche confederata*, who build their bungalows in different styles, are represented in the drawings which illustrate the story. Keti, himself, made his home on a southern holly (*Ilex*); but there are other kinds of leaves he would have liked as well. Sometimes, indeed, so many of these caterpillars build their cabins in an orange-grove that they bother the orange man, and then he has to get them out. This story first appeared in the *Ladies' Home Journal* for December, 1919. In connection with it the following references will be found useful.

Julia P. Ballard. *Among the Moths and Butterflies.* (G. P. Putnam's Sons.) "Life in a Basket": pages 115-118.

J. Henri Fabre. *The Life of the Caterpillar.* (Dodd, Mead, & Co.) Chapters IX and X: "The Psyches."

William Hamilton Gibson. *Sharp Eyes.* (Harper & Brothers.) "The Curious Basket-Carriers": pages 292-298.

Henry C. McCook. *Tenants of an Old Farm.* (Fords, Howard & Hulbert.) "Housekeeping in a Basket": pages 377-399.

Mary E. Murtfeldt and Clarence Moores Weed. *Stories of Insect Life.* (Ginn & Co.) "The Bagworm": pages 69-72.

www.ingramcontent.com/pod-product-compliance
Lightning Source LLC
Chambersburg PA
CBHW031850090426
42741CB00005B/428